D0820257

GOLF

HEAVEN

GOLF
HEAVEN

INSIDERS REMEMBER
THEIR FIRST TRIP TO

AUGUSTA

NATIONAL GOLF CLUB

●

EDITED BY JOHN ANDRISANI

Thunder's Mouth Press
New York

GOLF HEAVEN:
Insiders Remember Their First Trip to Augusta National Golf Club

Copyright © 2007 by John Andrisani

Published by
Thunder's Mouth Press
An Imprint of Avalon Publishing Group, Inc.
245 West 17th Street, 11th Floor
New York, NY 10011
www.thundersmouth.com

AVALON
publishing group incorporated

All rights reserved. No part of this publication may be reproduced or transmitted in any form or by any means, electronic or mechanical, including photocopy, recording, or any information storage and retrieval system now known or to be invented, without permission in writing from the publisher, except by a reviewer who wishes to quote brief passages in connection with a review written for inclusion in a magazine, newspaper, or broadcast.

Library of Congress Cataloging-in-Publication Data is available.

ISBN-10: 1-56025-788-1
ISBN-13: 978-1-56025-788-2

9 8 7 6 5 4 3 2 1

Interior design by *Ivelisse Robles Marrero*

Printed in the United States of America
Distributed by Publishers Group West

I dedicate this book to the members of Augusta National for once giving me the opportunity to realize my dream of visiting their outstanding club and playing the best darn golf course in America.

CONTENTS

Acknowledgments

WRITING A NONINSTRUCTIONAL book about golf was a new challenge for me, particularly because of the subject matter: the Augusta National Golf Club, in Augusta, Georgia. Whether you are a veteran golfer or a novice, you know that Augusta is the site of the prestigious Masters Tournament, played every April on Augusta National's pristine and super-challenging championship course. Surely, too, you also watch the exciting event on television, dreaming of one day being able to step foot on this historical place whose existence owes so much to the great golfer Bobby Jones. I once shared the same dream, and fortunately it came true for me, as it did for the other golfers. They tell their exciting, entertaining, humorous, heartwarming stories in this book, either in the first person or through me, based on my conversations with them.

The idea for *Golf Heaven* was conceived by the editorial staff at Thunder's Mouth Press, whom I thank for giving me the opportunity to relive my Augusta experiences in these pages.

I also thank my agent Farley Chase, of The Waxman Agency, in New York City, for taking care of all business matters.

My own story about my Augusta National experience is just one of twenty-eight, which is my way of saying that had it not been for the other passionate golfers, from varying working worlds, there would have been no book. It was a special pleasure when the late Bing Crosby's son Nathaniel relived his visit to Augusta. That story and every story in this book is great, and I'm grateful that I can share them with you.

INTRODUCTION

I BEGAN PLAYING golf in 1957, at the age of eight, and by the time 1964 rolled around my parents had purchased a junior membership for me at the Bellport Country Club in Bellport, on Long Island.

The Bellport course was designed by Seth Raynor, one of golf's finest course architects, and was laid out in a spectacularly scenic location on land that was ideal for a golf course. I especially liked hole number 10, a short par-3 that let you get a glimpse at the Great South Bay. Even better was hole 11, a very long par-3, about 230 yards, that featured a big dune to the right of the entranceway to the green. I loved standing on that green, and on the tee to hole 12, a par-5, watching sailboats gliding by in the wind and clam diggers pulling their rakes in, then dumping their catch into big burlap bags that were stacked on their funny-shaped thick wooden boats. At those moments in time, life in all its simple natural beauty was caught in a frame. I suppose, looking back, that it was then that my love for art and the aesthetic in general must have been nurtured and ingrained forever in my subconscious. I say that knowing this: I was extremely competitive, although playing golf at Bellport and at other courses with beautiful settings became as important as shooting a good score. Playing golf on a layout near water or one cut out of thick woods served as a catalyst in my becoming passionate about the game and set the standard for how, in the future, I would rate golf courses.

Bellport Country Club, still around today and a spectacular little gem, was also run very efficiently, by such colorful folks as Charlie Carter, the original pro, then Nick Petrillo, who took his place; Joe, the course superintendent; and Jimmy, the locker man, a real character who loved to play cards, drink with the boys, and play the horses.

Growing up in the 1950s and 1960s, I was totally absorbed in golf—even though it was considered by many to be a sissy sport—and I played practically every day during the summer months. I became so absorbed in golf that when not playing I read about the game in books and magazines and watched every golf show, including Shell's *Wonderful World of Golf* and *Big Three Golf*.

Back then there was no such thing as the Golf Channel, a round-the-clock channel; if there had been such a thing I would have been glued to the television even more often than I was and never would have completed my homework. What could be seen, however, was the telecast of the

Masters Tournament, played every April at the Augusta National Golf Club in Augusta, Georgia. Because this event coincides with the splendor of springtime and the virtual start of the golf season, particularly in the Northeast, it has always carried more weight and importance than the other three major championships: the United States Open, played in June; the British Open, in July; and the PGA (Professional Golfers' Association) Championship, in August. The Masters is the only one of the four major championships that is played at the same venue each year. That is why it has always remained the highlight of my golf calendar, and probably yours, too.

My passion for golf grew as the clock ticked away, and I completed my high school and college years, after which I turned professional; later, when I regained my amateur status and went to work as an editor at *Golf Illustrated* magazine, in London. I often fantasized of realizing one of my lifetime dreams: to visit Augusta. My desire to one day visit Augusta grew stronger after Bill Robertson, my editor at *Golf Illustrated*, returned to our office, just off Fleet Street, after a trip to Augusta, and I asked him to describe the experience. His response: "It's like going to church."

I had no idea what Bill meant by his comment. However, I did know one thing: the Augusta National Golf Club had a reputation for being the best-run darn golf club in the United States, and its course, I was told, was the most superbly manicured and stunningly beautiful inland "track" in the world. Having since played that course, I now know how right all those golf experts were about its greatness.

Unlike great courses such as Pebble Beach in California and St. Andrews in Scotland, Augusta is not open to the public—on the contrary, it is the most private club in the world, one that you join only by invitation of the members, and that's that. In fact, it's nearly impossible even to get inside the gates of Augusta to watch the game's best professionals compete in the Masters. That is precisely why every golfer longs to set foot on this sacred ground, just once.

When it comes to joining the Augusta National, I've been assured that no strings can be pulled or politics played to get exceptions made, and being rich or famous in no way guarantees an invite to join this most prestigious of golf clubs. Millions of golf enthusiasts around the world can only fantasize about being allowed to pass through the guarded entrance to the club, to drive down the long, fabled, tree-lined Magnolia Lane, to enter the historical clubhouse filled with Masters memorabilia, to wear one of the green sports coats given to members, and to play the wonderfully beautiful and challenging championship course with its pristinely green carpetlike fairways and greens surrounded by supremely colorful azaleas and dogwoods. It is a course like no other, dreamed up by the legendary Bobby Jones and designed by the famous architect Alister MacKenzie.

The Augusta membership committee has never cared about making money from advertising during the Masters Tournament, which is not the case with other major golf events. Augusta takes pride in running the greatest championship in the world, on what they consider the finest golf course, all for the benefit of their patrons, who love watching professional golfers compete for the coveted green jacket presented ceremoniously each year to the winner.

I would not go so far as to say that the members of Augusta National are like Augustus Caesar and his friends, who hosted one-on-one fight-to-the-death events in the Coliseum just for their own enjoyment and that of the screaming Roman crowds. However, during Masters week, members can be seen sitting back in *their* clubhouse sipping a mint julep, out on the course being entertained by the grand spectacle of the greatest golfers in the world hitting spectacular shots that trigger loud applause, or listening to the oohs and ahs of the gallery as one of Augusta's hazards gets the best of a player who gambled in going for a sucker-pin, failed to hit the perfect shot, and suffered the consequences. While the members enjoy themselves watching the tournament taking place at their club, the rest of the world's golfers must content themselves with watching the event unfold on television, hoping that one day they may be able to visit the club, either to watch the event or, better yet, play the course.

In 1983, a year after leaving England and returning to New York to work on Madison Avenue as instruction editor for *Golf Magazine*, I finally made it to Augusta on assignment. The split second I entered the gates and drove down Magnolia Lane toward the clubhouse, knowing the course was right behind it, I felt my heart beat faster. In the morning, walking the entire course before play began, I did, indeed, feel as though I was in church. Going from hole to hole, walking where the greats had walked, and taking in the gorgeous scenery surrounding the entire course, I felt the same sense of being tied to a higher power that I felt when I walked into Notre Dame Cathedral in Paris for the very first time.

One year later, in 1984, I was lucky enough to play Augusta National. The experience was wonderfully spiritual.

To appreciate the Holy Spirit, you must appreciate the life of Jesus Christ—his suffering, sacrifices, and the supernatural qualities that set him apart. By the same token, to appreciate why the Augusta National Golf Club stands alone in the world of golf, you must appreciate its history; how it was born, how it grew, and how it has managed to remain on the highest of pedestals. This story will be told through my words and those of other golfers who have been fortunate enough to realize their own dream of visiting the club to watch the Masters Tournament and even of playing the course.

Because of my career as a golf writer, I have had the opportunity to play golf at some of the greatest courses around the world, and Augusta is always on the minds of professional and amateur golfers. The only difference is that many pros have played Augusta, whereas only an infinitesimally small number of weekend golfers have ever visited, let alone played, this renowned club.

Golfers I have spoken to at public and private courses tell me every day that the Masters is the most entertaining of all tournaments to watch. However, they also tell me that when the tournament is over, they are left with an empty feeling in their stomachs, and not just because they know they have to wait another year to watch the next telecast but also because throughout the event, the colorful commentary sticks strictly to the golf being played. Reporters do not talk about the Augusta National Golf Club or what goes on behind closed doors, giving some golfers I've spoken to over the years the impression that Augusta is kind of a "secret-society" type club. Frankly, those are harsh words. Having met some of the gentlemanly members, I respect their right to remain private and their desire to refrain from talking about the everyday goings on inside the sacred grounds of their club.

Of course this strict privacy policy is perfectly understandable; nevertheless, because of it, many questions have gone unanswered. Therefore I am happy to be able to assure you that after reading parts one and two of *Golf Heaven* and the intimate, extraordinary, untold stories recounted therein by me and other individuals who managed to visit the Augusta National Golf Club, many, if not all, of your questions will be answered; albeit it, unquestionably, only in the most discreet manner.

PART

ONE

CHAPTER 1

THE MAKING OF A MASTERPIECE

John Andrisani

TO MILLIONS OF golf enthusiasts the world over, Augusta National Golf Club is a surreal fairyland in which every hole presents a picture-postcard setting, particularly in April, when the flora that surrounds the championship course is in riotous bloom and the game's most talented players compete for the coveted green jacket awarded to the winner of the Masters Tournament.

When Augusta National is on full display during Masters week, it is without question the Mecca of championship golf. Everything about this wonderful southern club—from the impeccably manicured course and practice areas to the like-home-type clubhouse with black shutters and giant old oak tree in its yard, to the caddies dressed in snow white uniforms, to the wide choice of delectable food, to the perfectly prepared cocktails, to the gorgeous flowers, to the polite, polished, professional staff, to the gentlemanly Augusta committee members, who, attired splendidly in their green jackets, walk around keeping everything running super-smoothly, just as founding club chairman, Clifford Roberts, hoped would happen.

Given the club's idyllic perfection today, it may surprise you to learn that aesthetically and financially Augusta National Golf Club has endured more than its share of growing pains since its birth. As has been well documented, the club itself and the Masters Tournament event teetered on the brink of extinction not just once but several times during the club's first dozen years of existence. This is one of the chief reasons why Augusta has such an unmatchable character—which, I'm told the club works arduously to retain through stringent rules: every single member obviously realizes how much blood, sweat, and tears went into creating Augusta, and thus do everything in their power to maintain this wonder of the golfing world.

For golfers, understanding how Augusta was born, grew to mammoth proportions, established itself as the most private and most well run club in America, and has retained its place at the top in a world where new expensive and luxurious country clubs are popping up every day is comparable to artists learning how the likes of Pablo Picasso and Claude Monet developed as artists and kept moving forward. You need to study the early works of these masters and follow their progress as they evolved; otherwise you will just look at a cubist painting by Picasso and brush it off as merely angles of pigment on canvas, or an Impressionist painting by Monet and see it simply as lilies of oil floating on water.

Like Picasso's and Monet's works, Augusta did not become a masterpiece overnight, but developed over time, moving constantly with the style of the day but holding on to traditional values, too, just as Picasso and Monet retained their basic sense of light and color, yet developed subtly new brushstroke techniques to produce works that will forever impress. The Augusta National Golf Club has been doing that for a long time, thanks to the likes of Bobby Jones—the great amateur whose story will allow you to start getting some answers to your questions so that you can begin to really appreciate that Augusta members are not snobs, but, rather, are simply damn proud of what they built and have today.

BOBBY JONES BUILDS HIS DREAM COURSE

The year 1930 was the finale of an eight-year stretch in which the world of golf was dominated by Robert Tyre Jones, Jr., now known as Bobby Jones. That was the year in which Bobby, then twenty-eight, captured all four of what were then golf's major championships: the British Amateur, the British Open, the U.S. Open, and the U.S. Amateur. Since winning the U.S. Open at Long Island's Inwood Country Club in 1923, Jones captured an astonishing thirteen championships in just twenty-one starts.

Clearly, after taking the Grand Slam, or the "impregnable quadrilateral," as it was sometimes called, Jones had no further worlds to conquer in competitive golf. Nor was it a realistic option for Jones, a lifelong amateur, to turn professional. In the first place, there was no year-round professional golf tour yet in place in 1930. Second, at that time golf professionals were relegated to second-class citizenship and considered "the help" by members of most country clubs. Third, Jones, with degrees in civil engineering, English, and law from Georgia Tech, Harvard, and Emory University, respectively, figured to earn far more in the business world than he could in those "pass the hat" days of professional golf. Fourth, in late 1930 Warner Brothers signed Jones to make golf instructional films, and shortly after that, A. G. Spalding paid him a six-figure salary—really unheard of in those days—to design and promote their golf clubs.

Last, and perhaps not least, the strain of playing championship golf had exacted a tremendous toll on Jones's nervous system. Though he always appeared calm and in control of his emotions during highly regarded tournaments, inside his stomach was constantly churning. The pressure reached such overwhelming heights that, in 1930, Jones retired after the U.S. Amateur, when he was at the pinnacle of his game.

During the late 1920s, Jones had often stated his desire to build a championship golf course in the South. Jones had also, during this period of his life, befriended a Wall Street stockbroker named Clifford Roberts. Roberts had connections to Augusta, Georgia, a small city of some 90,000 just west of the Georgia–South Carolina state line, where he had occasionally vacationed and where he had been stationed during the final months of World War I. Late in 1930, Roberts alerted Jones to the availability of a 365-acre farm that included a sprawling house overlooking the rolling property—today that structure serves as Augusta National's clubhouse. The property had been formerly owned by the Berckmans family of Belgium who, beginning in 1858, had developed it as a horticultural farm called Fruitland Nurseries. (Many of the flowering plants for which Augusta National is now world-famous were not native to this country but are descended from Fruitlands stock. In particular, the company advertised about a hundred different varieties of azaleas.) However, after the principal owner, Prospèr Berckmans, died in 1910, the farm gradually fell into disrepair, and it had lain fallow for some fifteen years.

When Jones first viewed the huge parcel, he was entranced by its possibilities, believing that the land was ideal for creating a golf course on. Jones also liked the location, because although it was moderately close (150 miles) to his hometown of Atlanta, Augusta was situated at a much lower altitude, so its climate was milder during the winter months. So, with all these positives inducements in mind, in January 1931, a group of business partners that included Bobby's father, Colonel Robert P. Jones, purchased the site.

In 1929, Jones had won the U.S. Open at Winged Foot but had been upset by Johnny Goodman in the first round of the U.S. Amateur Championship at Pebble Beach. This meant that he had some time on his hands, and Jones took the opportunity to play a new course in the area known as

Cypress Point. The architect of this spectacularly beautiful California course was Alister MacKenzie, a physician of Scottish origin. Jones, greatly impressed by Cypress Point, hired MacKenzie to design (with Jones as partner and consultant) the yet-unnamed course that would become Augusta National.

It fell to Clifford Roberts to develop Augusta's membership, and he began the task in the spring of 1931.

Roberts, who idolized Jones, believed that golfers nationwide would line up to join a golf club developed by the day's greatest and most popular player. What he didn't count on was the economic hailstorm known as the Depression. Just getting eighteen holes built was a stretch, although after the work began, in February 1932, the course was completed in around four months. To help construction along, MacKenzie reportedly reduced his design fee. MacKenzie last saw Augusta in the spring of 1932; in January 1934, he died suddenly after a brief illness, having never seen the completed Augusta masterpiece.

So much has been written about the greatness of Alister Mackenzie, and rightfully so, for he was certainly a brilliant golf course architect. However, as far as his work on Augusta National goes, in my opinion his design efforts overshadow those of Bob Jones, which I do not think is fair based on what I discovered; something that no one else has mentioned in any of the numerous well researched, superbly written books about Augusta National—most notably, *The Making of the Masters* by David Owen, *The Augusta National Golf Club* by Sam Byrdy, and *The Masters* by Dawson Taylor. Surprisingly, not even Jones mentions what I'm about to tell you in his autobiography, *Golf is My Game* (1960), when talking about "the land that had been waiting to have a golf course (Augusta) built on it." However, in *Down the Fairway*, the book he wrote thirty years earlier, he provides a hint as to what inspired his design ideas for Augusta National when he calls the Whitfield Estates golf course in Sarasota Florida, "one of the best in America."

In 1926, at age twenty-four, Jones played Whitfield Estates frequently while selling real estate part-time and living in Sarasota. This wonderful course, since renamed Sara Bay, was designed by golf's architectural genius Donald Ross, who also created Pinehurst Number 2 in North Carolina, another favorite of Jones, and, too, Seminole in Palm Beach, Florida.

Having been a member of Sara Bay, I see strong similarities between it and Augusta National, particularly the features of elevated greens, featuring slopes and crowns that reward pinpoint approach shots and run errant shots into collection areas or bunkers bordering the greens. The secret to going low on a Ross course is to hit the ball to the part of the green that leaves you a fairly level putt.

Playing the Whitfield Estates course encouraged Jones to develop a controlled driving game. It also forced him to make distance control a priority on iron shots into the green, and to hone a polished short game that was necessary when finding the ball in one of those treacherous collection areas and facing a short pitch, delicate chip, or curving putt; that is, if the ball did not roll back into one of the creeks that meander through the course and jut close to the greens on such holes as number four, five, eight, twelve, and eighteen.

Jones, along with the first golf professional at Whitfield Estates, Tommy Armour, liked this course so much that he invited other fine golfers to play it, most notably pros Jim Barnes and Johnny Farrell. Jones also played against Walter Hagen in an exhibition match at this posh Sarasota club, where baseball greats Babe Ruth and Dizzy Dean liked to visit in the winter months.

Why I bring up Jones's affection for the Whitfield Estates course, and also Pinehurst, is that although MacKenzie gets virtually all of the credit for designing Augusta National, it is obvious from the final creation— with its tree-lined fairways, elevated crowned greens, strategically placed bunkers, and manicured collection areas bordering the putting surfaces—that Jones played a major role rather than minor role in designing the course that is home to the Masters. It's obvious, too, that Jones was influenced much more than has been told, by Donald Ross, who as MacKenzie possessed the golf pedigree of being born in Scotland, where links golf was prevalent and the game was popularized. Furthermore, Ross had a style all his own, which to me is the one that Augusta National most resembles.

SITE OF A NEW TOURNAMENT

By Spring of 1933, Augusta National was teetering on the verge of bankruptcy. However, the ingenuity of Clifford Roberts saved the day. He proposed that Augusta National begin hosting its own tournament, that eventually became the Masters. While a new tournament could not hope to match the prestige of a USGA (United States Golf Association) event, it would still bring in publicity and revenue.

Roberts communicated with the Professional Golfers' Association of America (PGA), which then oversaw a tour of sorts that ran mainly through the winter months: this was the off-season, when club professionals from the Northeast and Midwest had time to compete. Augusta National was added to the PGA event schedule for March 22–25, 1934.

Technically, the Masters was not really the Masters in 1934, nor for several years thereafter. It was the Augusta National Invitational Tournament. Roberts had wanted to call it the Masters, but Jones believed that name to be too presumptuous.

SARAZEN'S MASTERS-SAVING STROKE

Despite the relative success of the first Augusta National Invitational, it has been well documented that the fortunes of the club remained in dire jeopardy for the remainder of the 1930s. Memberships remained down because of the strangling effects of the Depression, and for the next several years the tournament itself teetered on the edge of extinction, principally because the size of the Invitational's field of players gradually decreased. The problem was that the purse had remained the same since the inaugural event; it would not increase until after the 1942 tournament. Very few competitors could afford a trip to Augusta, which would give them little chance to break even on their expenses. So, even though they may have wanted to play and wanted to support Bobby Jones, his tournament, and his course, a dwindling number could afford to do so.

Against this gloomy backdrop, the tournament experienced amazing piece of good fortune in 1935, its second year. That April, Gene Sarazen, arguably the world's top player now that Jones had ceded the throne, hit what is known as "the shot heard 'round the world" at Augusta National. Trailing the leader, Craig Wood, by three strokes late in the final round, Sarazen faced a 230-yard second shot on the par-5 15th hole. The shot needed to carry the large pond fronting the green and, ideally, also hold the firm, fast-running putting surface.

Sarazen decided to go with his four-wood, toeing the club in just a shade to give the shot more distance, and swung. His strategy worked wonders, as the shot not only hit the green, but went into the hole for a double-eagle score of 2.

In the early 1980s, I actually spoke to Sarazen when interviewing him for a *Golf Magazine* feature on golf's greatest shots. Gene told me that on the day he hit his miracle shot, there were at most twenty-five golf enthusiasts in his gallery on a wet and chilly late afternoon, but that over the years about 20,000 people had told him they had seen the shot. Sarazen's miraculous shot wiped out Craig Wood's seemingly insurmountable advantage with one magical stroke. The little man known as "The Squire" managed to par the final three holes, forcing a playoff the next day, which he won.

According to Sarazen, Clifford Roberts told him that his double eagle, and the wave of publicity it generated, put the

Masters in business. If that's true, perhaps Roberts was overstating the shot's impact. All the same, Sarazen's shot did bring attention to the club.

In 1939, for the first time ever, Augusta National's membership count topped the one hundred mark. The gate also set a record that year, topping for the first time that of 1934, when fans had flocked to see Bobby Jones return to competition. The tournament had been officially dubbed the Masters in 1938, when Jones finally gave in to pressure from Roberts, the public, and the press on that score. Perhaps even a greater cause of optimism was the hatching at about this time of a new triumvirate of golf stars: Byron Nelson, Sam Snead, and Ben Hogan, who were to dominate the game until Arnold Palmer's arrival in the late 1950s. Nelson was the first of the three to blossom, when he captured the 1937 Augusta event.

Then, in September 1939, Hitler invaded Poland, and the world was turned upside down. Jones and Roberts were determined to continue with the Masters as well as all other club activities for as long as possible. In the case of the Masters, that turned out to be the spring of 1942, four months after Pearl Harbor and the United States' official entry into the war.

It was inevitable, though, that after the 1942 Masters won by Byron Nelson, Augusta National would have to shut down for the duration of the war, since travel had become very difficult, and many of the club's members and employees were by now enlisted in the armed forces. Many assumed that there would never be another Masters, and that the club itself might never open again. They were wrong!

THE MASTERS LEGEND GROWS
(AND IS OUTFITTED IN A GREEN JACKET)

Once World War II had ended and the U.S. economy once again was booming, Americans found that they had more time to enjoy leisurely pursuits, and golf was one of the foremost among them. Augusta National and the Masters, which had managed to keep themselves on the map during the Depression due to the tireless efforts of Jones and particularly of Roberts, now found themselves to be the beneficiaries of a new wave of popularity. In addition to the spectacle of the Masters competition itself, it seemed that there was always some new innovation to capture the fancy of a sportswriter who would then broadcast it to golf fans the world over. These innovations have served to lend the Masters an aura of tradition that makes the tournament seem to be much older than it really is. In reality the Masters is the youngest of today's four major golf championships; The oldest of the four is the British Open (1860); second is the U.S. Open, inaugurated in 1895, third is the PGA (1916) and the Masters brings up the rear, in 1934,

There is nothing on the record, at least to my knowledge, to verify who in particular should be credited with the notion to award the Masters winner a green jacket. However it came to be, the first version of the green sports jacket was worn by club members at the 1937 Masters. Roberts encouraged members to wear "coats," as he called them, as it would make them stand out, so that spectators could seek out a person of authority who could answer questions about a favorite player's tee time, direct them to a particular hole, provide them with a score update, and so forth.

It has been noted that members were unenthusiastic about wearing the first jackets, because in the original version they were made of 100 percent wool. According to Richard Donovan, renowned delaer of golf books, the original jackets were manufactured by Haskett in New York City. Apparently, too, over the years different companies have manufactured them, most notably one in the Midwest and though I know its name, I'd rather not mention it because as I understand they are still making the coats for Augusta, and I would sure not want to do anything that could harm this great tradition. I can tell you one anecdote a little birdie passed on to me. The company's owner has attended numerous Masters.

Today's green jacket, I've been told, is a blend of 50 percent wool and 50 percent polyester. The jacket itself is a three-button, single-breasted affair and its green color seems to match the color of the course's impeccable rye-grass fairways. The distinctive emblem on the left breast pocket shows the Augusta National logo, a map of the United States within an embroidered circle, with a flagstick and a cup placed at the site of the tournament. According to a former colleague of mine at *Golf Magazine*, these badges are manufactured by a company in the southern United States, and that's all I'm going to say. The jacket's brass buttons, which also display the Augusta National logo, are made by a company in the Northeast and that's all I'm going to say.

All Augusta National members I've heard are required to

purchase a green jacket. In keeping with the air of privacy
for which the Augusta National Golf Club is famous, members may, I understand, only wear their jackets on the
grounds of the club. In fact, in keeping with club policy,
they may not even take their jackets home; rather, the gar-
ments are stored in a large cedar closet within the clubhouse.

I've been told by George Peper, who for years wrote a
book annually on the Masters Tournament, that specific
comments about Augusta National, its policies, or the tournament are to be made only by the current club chairman.
When they are away from the club, members are even
advised not to boast about their play on the fabled course.
In summary, members are advised that *whatever occurs at
the club stays at the club*—just as the jackets stay in the cedar
closet on the premises. Personally, I respect such a policy.
It's the way things should be at a true private club.

It was not until 1949 that a green jacket was awarded to
the Masters winner. The first recipient was Sam Snead, who
was so honored after the first of his three wins. One time
when I was on a trip with him to Finland (where he gave a
golf exhibition at midnight) and he was reminiscing, he
assured me that getting the jacket was a surprise and gave
him the feeling that he had finally made it.

The presentation of the green jacket quickly became legendary. Today it is probably the greatest symbol of victory
in the world of sports, grander even than the yellow jersey
of the Tour de France or the garland of roses for the Kentucky Derby winner. Since 1949, the tournament winner
has been presented with his jacket by the previous year's
winner. There have been only three repeat winners: Jack

> **Green-Jacket Exceptions**
>
> Jack Nicklaus is the one player who has been granted a second green jacket. The Masters administrators allowed this when Nicklaus wanted to put his original green jacket on display at the Jack Nicklaus Museum in Ohio, which goes to show that if you happen to win the Masters six times, Augusta National's powers-that-be may very well cut you some slack.

Nicklaus (1965; 1966), Nick Faldo (1989; 1990), and Tiger Woods (2001; 2002). In 1966 Nicklaus donned the jacket himself, but it was presented by the tournament chairman, according to long-standing tradition, to Faldo and Woods. Today the ritual is carried out before the television cameras in Augusta's Butler Cabin, which is command central for the tournament telecast.

The ironic thing is even Masters champions are not allowed to keep their jackets. They are accorded possession of the green jacket for just one year, with the provision that it be worn only at golf-related events or social gatherings and be returned to the club at the next Masters. Multiple winners of the event receive the same coat over again, except that they receive another if their jacket size changes significantly between victories.

CHAMPIONS' DINNER AND OTHER MASTERS TRADITIONS

Another tradition of the Masters was started in 1952, when the first champions' dinner was held. Ben Hogan was the defending champion that year. He proposed that the defending champion host a dinner for past winners, an idea that was instantly embraced by Jones and Roberts. Ever since, the dinner has been held on the Tuesday evening before the tournament commences, and only past champions, the tournament chairman, and a photographer may attend. Each year the defending champion of the Masters Tournament gets to choose the dinner's main course. (The defender also picks up the tab for the dinner.) Now and again there have been some unusual choices. After his first win in 1997, Tiger Woods, then just twenty-two and still reasonably fresh from his college experience (and perhaps not yet fully comfortable with his sudden wealth), treated the Masters champs to cheeseburgers, French fries, and milkshakes. The defender in 2001, Vijay Singh, chose Thai cuisine, including chicken satay, chicken phanaeng kai, spicy shrimp, and baked sea bass.

Without a doubt, though, the most exotic and unpopular dish was the one the Scotsman, Sandy Lyle, selected in 1989. Lyle chose to serve haggis, a ghastly concoction of sheep's heart, liver, and lungs, which are minced and mixed with onions, oats, and herbs, stuffed in a sheep's stomach, and boiled. Fortunately, officials at Augusta National were prepared for the uncertain reaction and allowed the attendees to make alternate choices, for which most if not all were undoubtedly grateful.

Another innovation at the Masters is the Par-3 Tournament, which takes place every year on the Wednesday afternoon prior to the start of the main tournament at the club's short but also impeccably manicured nine-hole course. At that time, the competitors take part in a relaxed pre-tournament exhibition while the championship course is closed to practice and receives a final grooming.

The first Par-3 Tournament took place in 1960 and was

won by Sam Snead. This tournament quickly became a favorite offshoot event both for players and spectators. Interestingly, though, in the ensuing forty-six years, *no* winner of the Par-3 Tournament has ever gone on to win the Masters in the same year.

One other unusual tidbit regarding this lead-in event is that in 1990 Sam Snead tied for first place, at the ripe old age of seventy-eight.

Another feature that is unique to the Masters and adds to its great sense of tradition is the concept of honorary starters. These are players who strike the ceremonial first shots of the tournament and then, if they so choose, go on to play several holes.

The honorary starter concept at Augusta goes back to the two Scotsmen, Jock Hutchison and Fred McLeod, who had, respectively, won the 1937 and 1938 PGA Seniors Championships hosted by Augusta National for only those two years.

Hutchison and McLeod continued as honorary starters until 1973, and over the years some big names have carried on the tradition.

The club asked Gene Sarazen and Byron Nelson to continue the honorary-starters tradition, and in 1984 Sam Snead joined them, having competed in forty-four consecutive Masters.

At the time of this writing many avid Masters fans are wondering, when one or more of modern-day golf's Big Three (Arnold Palmer, Jack Nicklaus, and Gary Player) might assume the role of honorary starters at the Masters. Nicklaus, the youngest of the three, retired as an official competitor after the 2005 event—he was sixty-five—after

---

Oddities of the Augusta National Golf Club and the Masters Tournament

- After Gene Sarazen tied Craig Wood in 1935 on the strength of his famous double-eagle 2 on the 15th hole of the final round, Sarazen and Wood played a thirty-six-hole playoff the following day. Sarazen prevailed, shooting 144 to Wood's 149. Afterward, Clifford Roberts awarded Sarazen a $50 bonus for taking 108 holes to win the title, instead of just 72.

- It was thirty-two years before a second double eagle was made during the Masters. Bruce Devlin holed out a four-wood second shot at the 8th hole during the first round of the 1967 tournament.

- The Masters initiated a thirty-six-hole cut in 1957. (The low-40s players and ties and any players within ten strokes of the lead now survive the cut.) Gary Player became the oldest player ever to make the cut at the Masters in 1998, when he was sixty-two.

- Ben Hogan was always noted for his intense concentration when he competed. The story goes that in 1947 Hogan was paired with Claude Harmon (who would win the Masters the following year). At the par-3 12th hole, Hogan hit a fine shot to land the ball some twelve feet from the hole. Harmon, up next, made a spectacular hole-in-one. On the next hole, while walking down the fairway, Hogan commented to Harmon, "You know, Claude, that's the first time I ever birdied that hole." Some golf experts say this was the ultimate gamesmanship move, while others believe Hogan was in such a cocoon of concentration when playing in the Masters Tournament, that he never witnessed the ace!

continued on next page

---

shooting creditable rounds of 77 and 76. As of that date, Palmer was seventy-five and Player, seventy. If any of these legends appeared as honorary starters it would be another sizable chunk of lore that would help ensure the mystique of the Masters for decades to come.

- Sam Snead made what has to be the longest second putt in the history of golf at the Augusta National. During an early Masters, on the 5th hole, Snead stroked a fifty-foot putt from the huge green's lower level toward the hole on the top level. But his ball didn't quite get over the crest, and instead took a slow left turn and went rolling back toward the front of the green. Sam gave his second putt more steam, and this putt, estimated at sixty-five feet, went right in.
- One would think that among the members of the Augusta National, winning the club championship would be everyone's major goal and an honor to be savored for the rest of one's life. Surprisingly, though, *no* club championship is played at the Augusta National.
- It is well known that in 1968, Roberto DeVicenzo shot a final-round 65 but violated the rules of golf by signing instead for a 66. The added stroke knocked him out of a tie with Bob Goalby for the top spot.
- Nick Faldo is the only player in history to win two playoffs for the Masters title, in 1989, over Scott Hoch, and 1990, over Ray Floyd. And Ben Hogan is the only player to have lost two playoffs, in 1942, to Byron Nelson, and 1954, to Sam Snead.
- When Mark O'Meara birdied the 71st and 72nd holes to win the Masters by a single shot in 1998, he set a record for the most Masters attempts made by a player before winning—fifteen.
- Tickets to the first Masters Tournament (then known as the Augusta National Invitational) cost five dollars, plus fifty cents tax, and were good for all four days of the event.

How the Masters Became a Major

The Masters isn't a national championship like the U.S. Open or the British Open. Furthermore, it is not *the* tournament of American professional golf's official ruling body, the PGA Championship. Strictly speaking, the Masters is an *invitational* tournament that is run independently of any of golf's official ruling bodies, the United States Golf Association, the Royal and Ancient Golf Club of St. Andrews, or the Professional Golfers' Association of America. Furthermore, the Masters Tournament is by far the youngest of the majors—seventy-four years younger than the oldest, the British Open. So how did it gain its status and evolve into the most important of all major championships?

The short answers:

1. The charisma of Bobby Jones in drawing players and fans to the tournament in an era when golf was struggling mightily just to stay alive.
2. The incredible devotion on the part of Clifford Roberts to make the Masters the best-run golf tournament on the face of the earth.

Saying that a particular tournament is the best-run or simply the best covers a tremendous number of details and circumstances, of course. Let's examine some of these details more closely.

Perhaps the first point to mention is the timing of the Masters. Although the inaugural event was played in March, since the 1935 contest it has been played in early April, and has ended up on the second Sunday in April virtually every year since 1964. For the majority of the U.S. population living in the Northeast and Midwest, early April is the time of year when golfers are finally pulling their clubs out of their closets, garages, or basements after a long winter. Their thoughts are finely tuned in to golf at this time of year and they are at their most receptive to viewing the game's number one extravaganza, the Masters, because it coincides with the height of the blossoming period of an ornamental array of shrubs, trees, and flowers that grace the property, most notably dogwoods, azaleas, woodbine, redbud, daffodils, jasmine, camellias, and quite a few others. When the azaleas surrounding the rear of the 13th green at Augusta are in full bloom, they present what is arguably the most beautiful backdrop anywhere in golf.

In addition to the reputation of its sheer beauty, over the years Augusta National has become famous as the most impeccably manicured course in the world—thanks to top-class, expensive equipment and a first class team of experienced workers.

On a more technological note, believe it or not, the green at the par-3 12th hole, in the heart of the area of the course known as Amen Corner, has its own underground heating system. The 12th green, being in a heavily shaded area on the lowest part of the course, was susceptible to early-morning frost in the winter or early spring months, and thus could not be kept in the immaculate condition of the other greens. Some years back the club decided to have a system of pipes installed underneath that green, so that the temperature of the turf there is kept at a constant seventy degrees.

Augusta National is also pristine. Early on, Clifford Roberts decreed that at Augusta National there would be no "garbage," only "refuse." Never will you see items on the grounds such as sandwich wrappers (incidentally, wrappers of sandwiches sold at the club are Masters green in

---

Is It Real or Artificial Grass?

The result of the painstaking care that goes into preparing Augusta National for the Masters is sometimes too splendid for the first-time visitor to Augusta National to believe. I remember attending a Masters practice round one year, accompanied by an advertising client of *Golf Magazine* who had never been to the tournament.

We made our way through the admission gates, then past the clubhouse structures to a spot where a vista opens up on the high, rolling ground that overlooks the 1st tee, the practice green, the 9th and 18th greens, and other course features. The bright-green grass was a uniform texture and color all around. It was then that I noticed my guest looking down and brushing the tightly uniform mown turf with one foot. Finally he looked up at me and tentatively asked, "Is this real grass?" My response: "Yes, as in 'Ripley's Believe It Or Not.'"

This true story says it all regarding the perfectionism that characterizes the grounds keeping at Augusta National today.

---

color, of course) or any other type of "refuse." Many a player and fan has commented that for all the stately pine trees that line Augusta National's fairways, they can't remember ever seeing a pine cone lying on the ground! Although it's likely that here and there a fallen pine cone has actually entered a spectator's field of vision, workers are apparently lurking around the clock to keep the grounds as tidy as is possible at any given moment.

THE MASTERS AND TELEVISION

Another factor that has made the Masters unique is the manner in which it has maintained control of its television coverage, so as to present the public with a viewing product.

The first television broadcast of a professional golf tournament was in 1954, when the U.S. Open at Baltusrol Golf Club in New Jersey, was broadcast live by NBC. The network also retained the rights to broadcast the Masters, which Roberts fervently hoped it would do. But early in 1956, NBC, having reportedly lost money on that initial U.S. Open telecast, notified Augusta National that it would not renew its option to broadcast the Masters. Roberts countered this decision by NBC, by encouraging August to broadcast the Masters. Roberts countered this decision by NBC by encouraging Augusta to sign an agreement with CBS, and the first broadcast of the Masters took place the following year. CBS has broadcast the tournament ever since though along the way there were heavy negotiations between CBS and Roberts.

Thanks to Roberts, who I was told used to be served his favorite milk and Oreo cookies during meetings (but only ate the white icing), the telecast is essentially commercial-free, the transmission quality is superb because television cables are buried underground, and the tournament coverage is extensive; both in terms of time and holes we golf nuts get to see our favorite pros play.

AUGUSTA'S SUBTLE CHALLENGE

Augusta National is a prime example of what is known as "strategic" as opposed to "penal" architecture. During the 1920s, which was a golden age for golf architecture in this country, penal designs were more often the norm. This type of design tends to call for a great number of shots where the player has no option but to try to carry the ball

Arnie, TV, and the Masters

It was the club's good fortune—though it can be seen only on hindsight—that the rise of televised golf coverage coincided with the rise of golf's most beloved champion, Arnold Palmer, who would become the Masters' first four-time winner. (Arnold's record has since been surpassed by Jack Nicklaus's six victories, and Tiger Woods has already tied Palmer with his four wins in 1997, 2001, 2002 and 2005.

Palmer's first visit to Augusta National was in 1955. He had won the 1954 U.S. Amateur Championship, which qualified him to compete in the Masters. Palmer's debut was not terribly impressive. For the record, that year Palmer tied for tenth place—fourteen strokes behind the winner, Cary Middlecoff.

Three years later, in 1958, Palmer took his first Masters title.

The year 1960 was a watershed year for both Palmer and the tournament. After leading on the first day with a score of 67, Palmer

continued on next page

over deep bunkers, water, or fiendish rough. A strategic course, such as Augusta National, is more subtle. From the tee it may look wide open rather than penalizing, but depending on where the pin is located on a given hole, there is an optimum line of play for both the tee shot and the approach.

If a golfer strays somewhat on a strategic course such as Augusta National, pulling or pushing the drive slightly, to the untrained eye it may appear that he or she is still in fine shape. But the second shot may be much more difficult in that it may have to carry a knob at the front of the green, or land on a part of the green that runs away from the player so that the shot cannot hold the green. Having slowly lost his advantage and by day four found himself a stroke behind Ken Venturi on the 71st tee. Under intense pressure, Arnie holed a 27-foot birdie putt on hole 17 to tie Venturi. Then he electrified viewers nationwide by knocking his six-iron approach stiff on 18 and holing the putt, to snatch the title from the luckless Venturi.

The next year, Palmer, as defending champ, clawed back from four strokes behind Gary Player in the final round and strode down the 18th fairway with the lead and, it seemed, the tournament in the palm of his hand. From there, however, he pushed his approach into the right bunker, sailed his sand shot over the green and down an embankment, and made a double-bogey 6 that gift-wrapped the title for Player. Today, such a finish would be called a choke, but at the time, Palmer was so popular that the loss was considered more of a tragedy.

Palmer won his third Masters in 1962, beating Player and Dow Finsterwald in a three-way playoff.

In 1964, "Arnie" became the first four-time Masters winner, this time with a resounding six-stroke victory.

played the course, I can tell you it sure looks easy, but as you'll learn when you read my story and some by others too, it's a very difficult course to score on.

After Augusta National caught the attention of the public through the Masters, many course architects began to favor more strategic designs, which also tend to be more playable for the high handicapper than penal courses. Augusta National features relatively few bunkers, compared to other major championship venues.

Jack Nicklaus's own Muirfield Village in Dublin, Ohio, the site of the PGA Tour's Memorial Tournament, is a world-class strategic course whose design, Nicklaus readily admits, borrows greatly from the strategic principles of Augusta National.

But what truly strikes fear into the world's greatest players is Augusta's greens. Year in and year out, players and the golfing cognoscenti agree that the greens at Augusta National are the fastest in tournament golf. Augusta National has indeed set the standard by which the speed of greens at other prestigious golf courses is measured.

When you add together this type of speed with the considerable contours built into just about every putting surface, you have a lethally nerve-shattering challenge that can cause even the most pressure-tested pro to cower. It's like putting on giant, contoured pool tables, but with no railings to stop the ball. In fact, some golf experts think that the speed and the breaks in Augusta National's greens are just too much—that the tournament overemphasizes putting, and thus eliminates many great ball strikers from contention. Supporters like me claim that Augusta indeed rewards only the very best ball striking, meaning that a championship contender must place his approach shots with laser accuracy so that he leaves himself with fairly straight, uphill putts. I also point to the lengthening of the course and the addition of trees, which tighten several fairway landing areas, as evidence that Augusta National compares favorably with any other course in the world as a venue for a major championship and a complete test of the champs' capacities.

It should be added that many visitors who see Augusta National for the first time are surprised at just how hilly the course is. There is much more contouring to be dealt with than either photographs or views on television can reveal. For example, the 10th green is roughly one hundred feet lower than the teeing area. So players also have to factor uphill, downhill, and side-hill stances into their shot-making planning and execution.

Another way that Augusta National has influenced golf-course architecture is in the way the grass surrounding the greens is shaved to fairway length, rather than being raised as high rough. At first glance this might appear to make the course play easier, but that's not the reality. The tightly mown areas allow the shot that misses the green to keep rolling farther from the green, and often finish in a hollow. The player is obliged to decide among several options to play a delicate recovery shot: a soft lob, pitch-and-run, bump-and-run, or putt.

In recent years the Masters Tournament committee decided that instead of keeping the entire playing area essentially mowed as fairway, they would allow the still-broad fairways to be bordered by a very light cut of rough referred to as "second cut." Never mind that this second cut is lower and most certainly more uniform than the fairways at most public courses. What's important to realize is that this course feature poses an additional problem to the player who needs a tight, very clean lie to put maximum backspin on the ball on approach shots to the super-demanding greens. The slightly higher grass of the second cut reduces the shot's backspin, often making it impossible to stop the ball near the hole when it has been played from this second cut.

A PROFILE OF AUGUSTA NATIONAL

Perhaps one day you will be fortunate enough to visit or

play Augusta National, although the chances of this happening, as you know, are very slim. Therefore, to give readers a better feel for the stories in this book, as well as a guidebook when they are watching the Masters on television, I provide here a description of each of the eighteen holes: its name (each hole is named for a flower or plant that is found in abundance at Augusta); its current yardage and par; and a brief description. The total yardage and par for the course are 7,445 and 72, respectively.

The Outward Nine Holes (par 36; 3,735 yards)

Hole 1, Tea Olive: par 4, 455 yards

One of the recently lengthened holes, Tea Olive is a stern starter. It plays slightly uphill and usually into a prevailing breeze, with trees lining the left side and a fairway bunker down the right side. The preferred place to land the tee shot is the left center of the fairway. Most players try to favor the right side of the green with the approach. The green is full of subtle breaks, and two putts for par are gladly accepted.

Hole 2, Pink Dogwood: par 5; 575 yards

This hole has also been lengthened, but it is still one of the prime birdie opportunities on the course. It is a downhill, sharp dogleg to the left. A fairway bunker lurks at some three hundred yards out on the right, and the trees down the left must also be avoided, because the slope of the ground will usually send the ball even deeper into the woods. Those in good position off the tee face a long second shot off a downhill lie, to an extremely wide but shallow green. Hitting and holding the green in two is thus extremely difficult. Many birdies are made by getting the ball up and down from one of the two fronting bunkers.

Hole 3, Flowering Peach: par 4; 350 yards

The shortest par-4 on the course is no pushover. A nest of bunkers guards the left side of the fairway, with trees on the right. Most pros will hit an iron off the tee to lay up short of the bunkers. This leaves a pitch to a smallish green that sits atop a mound. If the pin is on the shallow left side, pinpoint distance control is needed to clear the mound in front, yet hold the putting surface. Some players take out a driver and try to smash the ball nearly to the green, and take their chances with a testy short-game shot to earn a birdie.

Hole 4, Flowering Crab Apple: par 3; 240 yards

This hole was designed to resemble Eden, the par-3 7th at St. Andrews, in Scotland, which was a hole much admired by MacKenzie. Year in, year out, the 4th is one of the toughest on the course in relation to par. The slightly downhill shot usually requires a long iron. It's desirable to keep the ball's flight below the tree line beyond the green; otherwise the wind may play havoc with the shot. A deep bunker guards the front-right of the green, and there is another to the green's left. The rear of the green is much wider than the front, but it slopes dramatically. A back-right pin placement is the toughest on this hole.

Hole 5, Magnolia: par 4; 455 yards

Hole 5 is the farthest away from the clubhouse, and so it

gets less attention than many others. Nevertheless it's a very difficult hole—even for top Tour professionals. A drive down the left side of this dogleg-left hole is ideal, because it shortens the hole and provides a better angle of approach to the diagonally shaped green. Unfortunately, two fairway bunkers threaten this line. There's room to drive out to the right but this leaves a longer iron shot from an angle that makes it very difficult to hit and hold the two-tiered putting surface. What is shocking—and you'll know what I mean if you ever play the course yourself—is that Jack Nicklaus eagled this hole not once but twice in 1995.

Hole 6, Juniper: par 3; 180 yards
This downhill shot to a large green looks deceptively simple. But the green slopes down sharply from back to front, with the front-left guarded by a deep bunker. So, it's difficult to hit this side of the green while keeping the ball below the hole. The higher right side of the green is fairly level, although in years past there was a huge mound there. If the pin is located right, it's best to miss the shot to the right and/or short, leaving a fairly straightforward uphill chip. Shots landing on the left half of the green when the pin is on the right make three putts the norm rather than the exception.

Hole 7, Pampas: par 4; 450 yards
Pampas, which played at 365 yards for many years, used to be a birdie hole, but now it's a bit tougher. This is the tightest driving hole at Augusta National, with tall pines lining both sides, so many pros opt for a three-wood here. This leaves most players an uphill short-iron shot to a

shallow green (only fifteen paces from front to back) that's ringed by five bunkers. The putting surface is not visible from where the players must hit their approach shots.

Hole 8, Yellow Jasmine: par 5; 570 yards
Though this uphill hole has been gradually lengthened, it can still be reached in two by the biggest hitters. However, to have a good angle to hit a shot to the green, which curls around a grove of trees on the left, the drive must skirt the large fairway bunker on the right side, or carry it about 300 yards in the air. Players who can't reach in two will lay up to the right, where there's a generous landing area. That leaves a fairly open pitch to a long, narrow green that features steep mounds on both sides.

Hole 9, Carolina Cherry: par 4; 460 yards
This downhill hole doglegs sharply left, but the fairway slopes from left to right, so a substantial draw is desirable to keep the tee shot in the fairway. A good drive leaves the pros with a middle iron off a slightly downhill lie, and back uphill to a green that slopes sharply from back to front. It's especially difficult to judge the distance on the approach correctly, and to stop the ball below the hole and avoid a lethal downhill putt. Pros consider a front-pin position the toughest here, even though the slope of the "false front" has been softened in recent years.

The Inward Nine Holes (par 36; 3,710 Yards)
Hole 10, Camellia: par 4; 495 yards
This dogleg-left hole generally plays shorter than its

mammoth length would suggest. A well-hit draw off the tee allows the ball to catch the steeply downhill, right-to-left slope, often adding some fifty yards to the drive. This might leave a six- or seven-iron approach from a desirable angle to this right-to-left-sloping green. A tee shot that hangs out to the right, however, leaves a very difficult long iron, from an angle that makes holding the green extremely tough. An approach that catches the right-hand bunker leaves one of the toughest short-game shots on the course.

Hole 11, White Dogwood: par 4; 505 yards
This is the beginning of the three-hole stretch known as Amen Corner, aptly named in 1957 by the acclaimed golf writer Herbert Warren Wind. The 11th hole has been much adjusted in recent years. In addition to being lengthened, it has had a grove of pines added down the right side, preventing players from hitting hard tee shots down the right with a hook for extra roll. A small pond eats into the left side of the green, forcing most players to err to the right on the downhill approach. In fact, Ben Hogan once said, "If you see my second on the green, you'll know I missed my shot." Ray Floyd lost his chance for a second green jacket here in 1990, when his second shot found the pond during a playoff with Nick Faldo.

Hole 12, Golden Bell: par 3; 155 yards
Even with its modest length, the 12th is a hole that scares the greatest golfers in the world. At the lowest point on the course, swirling winds wreak havoc with club selection. And choosing the correct club is a must, because the green, which

angles from left to right, is extremely shallow, with Rae's Creek and a bunker in front and two bunkers at the rear. If the flagstick is on the right, the margin for error is tiny. Arnold Palmer lost the 1959 Masters here when, in the lead, he made a triple-bogey 6 in the final round. Yet Fred Couples got the break of his career on the Golden Bell in 1992 when his tee shot hit the bank short of the right side of the green, yet somehow stopped rather than rolling into the water.

Hole 13, Azalea: par 5; 510 yards

Several years ago, the tournament committee purchased a parcel of land from the adjoining Augusta Country Club, for the express purpose of moving back the tee on this great, short par-5 (which had become too short for today's booming hitters). The ideal drive must be drawn around the trees on the left-hand corner. This will put the player within easy reach of the green on the second shot. However, Rae's Creek winds down the entire left side of the hole before cutting across the front of the wide, angled green. A drive that's hit to the safer right side usually forces the player to lay up, because the second shot is much longer and must be played from a severe side-hill lie. The ensuing pitch over the creek is still tricky after a lay-up.

Hole 14, Chinese Fir: par 4; 440 yards

The only hole on the course without a bunker, the dogleg-left 14th, on which the fairway slopes slightly right, is still difficult. That's mainly because of a massive mound that guards the front of the huge, wildly sloping green. The lofted approach is better off being long than short. Playing a chip from behind the green is not too difficult, but hitting one close to the hole from in front of the putting surface is extremely so.

Hole 15, Firethorn: par 5; 530 yards

The Firethorn is another dramatic birdie or eagle opportunity that's fraught with danger. Players planning to go for the green in two try to drive down the right side, although new trees have tightened the tee shot. The biggest hitters may have only medium irons into the green, but the second shot is demanding, particularly if the pin is on the left. The wide green is extremely shallow here, so it's possible to hit the water either short or long, as the pond at the par-3 16th hole is not far beyond. Gene Sarazen made his famous double eagle here in 1935.

Hole 16, Redbud: par 3; 170 yards

Originally Redbud was a 115-yard pitch across a diagonal branch of Rae's Creek, with the green sitting just left of where the pond is today. It was too easy, though, and in 1947 the hole was redesigned by the golf architect Robert Trent Jones. The hole is still fairly short, but now it is much more dangerous than before. The tee shot is now over a pond that winds around the left side of the green, with a bunker also on the left. Two more bunkers overlook the front- and back-right. The green has two levels, the right side being the high side and the left side being much lower. If above the hole, the player faces the fastest chip or putt on the course. A tough pin position is at the front-right: Even though this shortens the hole, the raised area of the green there presents a minute target.

Hole 17, Nandina: par 4; 440 yards
This uphill par-4 has been lengthened, so that the Eisenhower Tree (named that because Ike, a club member, struck it so many times), guarding the left side of the fairway gives today's players something to think about. After that, the fairway widens in the landing area, and the green is fairly roomy behind the two fronting bunkers. However, when the pin is on the right, many players, while trying to keep the ball below the hole, either catch the front-right bunker or see the ball slowly trickle down and off the front-right portion of the green. The back-left of the green also falls away from the player.

Hole 18, Holly: par 4; 465 yards
This uphill par-4 was always considered a challenging finisher, even *before* the tee was backed up a full sixty-five yards! The player must thread a drive through a long, frighteningly narrow chute, preferably with a slight fade that will keep it away from the massive bunkers about 300 yards out from the tee. Too much slice and the player is "dead" in the trees to the right. After a good drive, the Tour player is faced with a middle iron up to a deep, two-level green that's difficult to two-putt if he finds the wrong level. A miss to the right, in the large bunker there, leaves a better chance to get up-and-down than a miss to the left, where the ground slopes severely away.

A GLIMPSE INSIDE THE AUGUSTA NATIONAL GOLF CLUB
Those who enter the fabled club grounds—whether a professional prior to competing in the Masters, or a guest fortunate enough to have the opportunity to play the

fabled course—experience how the setting changes from everyday hubbub to a fairy-tale land of golf in an instant. The visitor approaches along Washington Road, which is the main street running through the small city of Augusta Georgia. Washington Road, being a main street, is jam-packed with commercial properties such as fast-food and pizza joints, gas stations and convenience stores, car repair shops, and the like. If said visitor isn't watchful, he or she may miss Augusta National Golf Club and the entrance to the club via Magnolia Lane; a 330-yard long, shady entranceway bordered by tall Magnolia trees.

Arnold Palmer has said that he still gets goose bumps every time he enters Magnolia Lane, and Gary Player told me that for years he felt a great deal of pressure the split second he drove down Magnolia Lane.

Magnolia Lane finally opens onto the flowing circular driveway that fronts the Augusta National clubhouse. Within the drive is an area of perfect, bright green grass, and within it is a bed of brilliant yellow pansies that form the shape of the United States. It's no wonder that I and many others who have visited this prestigious club, feel a strong sense of patriotism.

The main clubhouse building, just beyond the circular driveway, was the primary residence of the Berckmans family before the property was acquired by Bobby Jones's group. In fact, to remind one of this well-documented fact, gigantic wisteria vine, originally planted by the Berckmans family in the late nineteenth century is alive and well at the rear side of the clubhouse, where it climbs well up above the second-floor balcony.

Inside, the décor is understated. The clubhouse staff is so unobtrusive as to seem almost invisible. Yet it is uncanny how a waiter seems to appear at the very moment the visitor is thinking of ordering a drink, having lunch, or taking advantage of whatever service he might require. Although you don't hear very much about the epicurean benefit of being an Augusta National member, the food, as you might well imagine, is absolutely top of the line. Nobody brags of such things at Augusta National. You find out for yourself when you get there.

On the third floor of the clubhouse is the Crow's Nest, a small area that's partitioned into four sleeping quarters. Amateur qualifiers are offered the opportunity to lodge in the Crow's Nest throughout their stay, and most do. This allows them ample time to drink in the history and observe the tastefully displayed memorabilia, for example, in the upstairs library, the portrait of Bobby Jones following through on his swing. They might also try to sneak a peek at the display in the champions' locker room, which of course includes, among other items, a green jacket.

They have a way of doing things at Augusta National— the right way! I've been told that's been the policy since 1931, when Clifford Roberts became the club's founding chairman.

Roberts's influence has most certainly maintained a firm hold over policies at Augusta National long after his death by suicide in 1977. Stories abound about how Roberts took Jack Whitaker, a longtime Masters announcer and commentator, to task in the early 1960s for referring to highly enthusiastic fans of Arnold Palmer as "a mob." During the early 1990s, the colorful CBS commentator Gary McCord was dropped after he pretty much told television viewers that the greens were so fast that they must have been treated with "bikini wax." Those who know Gary, including me, know he meant no harm—but to this day during CBS's telecast of the Masters, McCord has never been back in the commentators' booth. Apparently, the Augusta National Golf Club members respect forever the way Roberts liked things to be done; again the right way

So You Want to Become a Member of Augusta National?

Persons who entertain the idea that they would like to become a member of Augusta National should be advised that the days when the club sent out simple membership application cards are now part of the ancient lore of the club. Today, people do not approach the Augusta National Golf Club and announce that they would like to become members. Rather, as I've been assured by in-the-know golf aficionados, the club, if it so chooses, will ask you to join.

Golf insiders that play Augusta as guests also assure me that being wealthy enough to afford to be a member is a meaningless qualification for being asked to join. It is my understanding that an individual must be someone who has shown a long-standing devotion to the game of golf, who has a reasonable modicum of ability to play the game, who has been an exemplary member of both society and commerce—and, of course, has the acquaintance of one or more current members of Augusta National who will recommend him to the membership committee. Even Bill Gates, the founder of

---

Cliff Roberts's Final Trip to Augusta

In 1977, Clifford Roberts was eighty-three years old and reportedly in such poor health that he chose to end his life, with a pistol shot to his temple, on the grounds of Augusta National; the place he really called "home."

In dealing with life's issues, we are taught to look forward, never back.

Ironically, in the case of Clifford Roberts, it's extraordinarily difficult not to look back at a lifetime of incredible achievements— contributions that greatly influenced the evolution of the Augusta National Golf Club as well as the Masters Tournament, and helped keep golf a gentlemanly game.

Even more ironic, Roberts was found near Ike's Pond, named after his dear friend and former President of the United States: Dwight D. Eisenhower.

Roberts's presence at Augusta National will forever be missed, but having visited this club of clubs, I can assure you that his spirit lives on inside the gates.

Microsoft, did not waltz into Augusta, I've been told, though I understand that he is now a member.

AUGUSTA NATIONAL'S MOST FAMOUS MEMBER

In April 1948, a visitor was invited to make a lengthy stay at Augusta National, a stay that in upcoming years was to prove highly beneficial to the visitor, and even more so to the club. The visitor was Dwight David Eisenhower, formerly chief of staff of the United States Army during World War II, and future president of the United States.

Clifford Roberts was more than delighted to have the general visit. Aside from the prestige factor that the club could gain from such an eminent individual, the fact of the matter was that Roberts idolized Eisenhower, just as he had idolized Bobby Jones over the previous two decades. Roberts could not do enough for Eisenhower; and for Eisenhower, who was an enormously popular war hero, Augusta National offered a sort of sanctuary from the constant attention of politicians, the press, and the general public. Roberts went to the extreme of ordering Pinkerton guards to provide security during Eisenhower's stay, and apparently no other guests were allowed to visit while Ike was there.

Not long after Ike's initial visit, he was invited to join the club, and he did so enthusiastically.

Eisenhower was exceedingly passionate about golf (even though he was a high handicapper) and bridge—sometimes playing the popular country club card game against friend and equally skillful opponent, Clifford Roberts, until midnight.

There's no doubt that Eisenhower's membership at Augusta National added significant stature to the club. The members of Augusta were so fond of Ike that, in 1953, they built a cabin for him, called the Eisenhower cabin, on the club's property, for his use (it is one of ten cabins). In fact, today, Eisenhower's desk and chair grace the clubhouse library.

MODERN-DAY ISSUES

In recent years, Augusta National has maintained what it perceives as its right to operate in the manner of its choosing, regardless of any outside political implications. A few years ago, the club and its former chairman, Hootie

Johnson (Billy Payne became Augusta's new chairman on May 21, 2006), came under heavy criticism for the lack of female club members. The complaint was filed by the National Organization for Women (NOW), spearheaded by its chairwoman, Martha Burk. In the months leading up to the Masters, editorials that appeared in major newspapers across the country took sides on the issue.

Hootie Johnson and the club members dug in their collective heels and stated flatly that no outside organization could force Augusta National to change its policies in any area. NOW, led by Burk, threatened to demonstrate at the Masters, and also made clear its disapproval of the tournament's corporate sponsors, who, it claimed, were by extension supporting what NOW considered policies unfair to women.

Finally, Johnson delivered the coup de grace regarding the entire issue by announcing that Augusta National would do without any corporate sponsors and fund the tournament by itself. With this bold stroke, the administration of Augusta National in effect told all interested parties that Augusta National and the Masters could not be arm-twisted nor bought out at any price.

NOW did mount a protest of the Masters, but local legal ordinances determined that any demonstrations would have to take place at a substantial distance from the club's grounds—well away from the flow of the tournament's patrons into and from the event. The Masters went off with barely a hitch. The editorials on the issue stopped running. And, as of this writing, Augusta stopped running National's policy on admitting women members remains unchanged.

AUGUSTA'S GENEROSITY

Despite its imperious ways, the administrators of the Masters make it their goal to treat their patrons royally. Each day's pairing sheets and a map of the course are distributed free of charge. The club's famous pimiento and cheese sandwiches in their green wrappers, as well as all soft drinks, are sold at extremely modest prices. Harking back to the efforts of Clifford Roberts, the club also continues to call on course architects to shape and re-shape the mounds that surround the greens and fairways on many of the holes so as to improve the patrons' viewing vantage points.

Masters patrons are encouraged to show sportsmanlike behavior while watching the tournament, and they do so, since no one wants to lose a regular ticket.

Augusta National's administrators also make it a point to reward its hard-working staff members for their dedication. According to Tripp Bowden, a former Augusta caddy and one of the storytellers in this book, the final week that the club is in operation each season, at the end of May, is known as Closing Week. During that week all employees, including greens-keeping staff, chauffeurs, cooks, waiters, locker-room attendants, and caddies, are allotted one day on which they are allowed to enjoy playing the fabled course, as well as the club's other amenities. The final day of the season is known as Caddy Day. Starting at the crack of dawn, Augusta's caddies are sent out in foursomes and each caddy is given his own cart. This allows and encourages them to play as many holes as they can on that one day.

Getting into the Masters

The Masters is probably the toughest ticket to obtain in sports, year in and year out. The tournament has been sold out for forty years running, since 1966. The mailing list of regular attendees has remained virtually constant, except when a person dies. But the deceased's immediate family remains in line for tickets.

I've never heard of any living person who has ever contacted the club and asked to be taken off the Masters ticket list. And there is no point at all in inquiring about being put on a waiting list for tickets in the future. The list is already so long that I've heard Augusta National stopped adding names to the list more than twenty-five years ago.

These days—thanks to the Augusta national course providing great theater, as well as the added excitement of watching the likes of Tiger Woods and Phil Mickelson do battle with their golf clubs— Augusta is a hot ticket. So hot that tickets to the practice rounds have no longer been made available to the general public on a first come, first served basis. Instead, a lottery held in advance, and only those individuals who are among the fortunate few (in addition to the regular patrons) who are selected may attend early in the week. The demand for tickets to the Masters Tournament is so great that ticket owners have been known to put their passes up for sale on the "black market," selling a week long badge for thousands of dollars; covertly, of course, through special events agencies.

Should you decide, despite these obstacles, that attending the Masters is something you just have to do once in your life, at any cost, be forewarned that both public and private lodging anywhere in the Augusta area will be booked very early, and will likewise carry an outlandish price-tag.

MODERN-DAY MASTERS HEROICS

In the course of recounting the history of Augusta National and the Masters, we have touched on some especially memorable performances up to and including those of Arnold

Palmer in his heyday. In the next section are more tales of what many consider the most exciting performances and individual shots that have been showcased since that time. All of these legendary exploits have helped to build up the popularity of this great venue.

1975: The Nicklaus-Weiskopf-Miller Shootout

In the mid-1960s, it was apparent that Arnold Palmer, for all his talent and charisma, could not stop Jack Nicklaus from taking over not only the role of the top player in golf, but also the top player at Augusta National, Palmer's favorite stomping grounds. Nicklaus was ten years younger than Arnie and was without a doubt the strongest hitter in the game up to that time. On top of that, the young Nicklaus was proving to be, if not statistically one of the game's best putters, then certainly one of the very best clutch putters, particularly when a major championship was on the line.

Nicklaus had taken his first green jacket in 1963, his second year as a pro. In 1965 he shattered Ben Hogan's record Masters score of 274 (shot in 1953) by posting a seventeen-under-par 271 total score while whipping the field by nine shots, also a record at that time. It was Nicklaus's performance in 1965, and particularly his ability to dominate Augusta National's par-5 holes, that prompted the great Bobby Jones to remark, "He plays a game with which I am not familiar."

Nicklaus had added two more titles in 1966 and 1972 and thus was tied with Palmer, each having four Masters victories to their credit. In 1975, Jack, now thirty-five, was at the zenith of his career. But in addition to combatting his older rivals such as Palmer, Billy Casper and Lee Trevino, he also had a couple of younger guns to hold off, namely Tom Weiskopf, and Johnny Miller. Weiskopf, who like Nicklaus had attended Ohio State and who finally appeared to be delivering on his enormous potential, had taken the British Open in 1973. Also in that year Miller, he of the blond, surfer-boy good looks, had set the U.S. Open single-round scoring record at Oakmont, with an astonishing 63 in the final round, to claim his first major title. Furthermore, in 1974, Miller— with laser-like iron shots that led to some incredible scoring—won eight tournaments and was the year's leading money winner. Both these players obviously had the game to win the Masters in 1975. Weiskopf especially dearly wanted a Masters win, having already tied for second three times.

During the first two days, the tournament appeared to be Nicklaus's in a walk. He fired opening rounds of 68–67 to open a five-stroke lead. Weiskopf was six behind, and Miller actually had to hustle to make the cut when he followed an opening 75 with a 71.

Saturday's third round was one of those magical days at Augusta National, when the roars for birdies and occasional eagles echoed over the hills and valleys of the fabled course. Most of those cheers were for Johnny Miller. Having played his front nine before the leaders even went out, Miller fired a record 30 on the front side, six under par. He was suddenly within range of Nicklaus's lead. For all Nicklaus's formidable powers of concentration and his ability to shake off his opponents' charges, he could not get the putts to fall this day and carded by far his worst round of the tournament, a one-over-par 73. Miller finished with a 65, which reduced his deficit to Jack from eleven strokes to three. But the big story late in the day was Weiskopf, who fired a six-under-par 66 and, by day's end, held the lead over Nicklaus by one.

On Sunday, Nicklaus was in the next-to-last twosome, just ahead of Weiskopf and Miller. These three quickly pulled away from the field, with Nicklaus and Weiskopf taking turns forging a lead while Miller trailed the two, but was never out of it. By the time Weiskopf birdied the 15th hole, he had once more taken a one-stroke lead.

Then, as Weiskopf and Miller watched from the 16th tee, Nicklaus faced a twisting, uphill forty-foot putt from the front-left of the green to the hole on the upper right. He stroked it firmly, watched intently as it climbed the hill and curved left. Nicklaus did a quick stomp around the green as the improbable putt dropped in the hole, and the crowd erupted. Back on the tee, Weiskopf is said to have murmured, "The son of a —— did it to me again."

Weiskopf then hit his iron fat, his ball just reaching the green, from where he three-putted to surrender the lead to Nicklaus. That's the way it stood going to the 18th hole. Miller sank a clutch birdie putt on hole 17 and also got within one.

Nicklaus, playing the percentages, made a safe par at hole 18 and waited to see if his younger rivals could catch him. Miller drove well and put a seven-iron on the heart of the green, some eighteen feet away. Then Weiskopf, having hammered a monstrous drive, wedged to just eight feet, on virtually the same line of putt as Miller.

Miller made a good stroke, but his putt swung sharply from right to left and missed the hole by a couple of inches on the low side. Weiskopf went to school on Miller's putt. He started his eight-footer just outside the hole on the right, waiting for the break—which did not quite come in time. The putt burned the top lip as it edged past; the dejected countenances of Weiskopf and Miller trudged off the 18th green. The moment was Jack Nicklaus's: he had survived, to win his record fifth Masters title.

1978: Gary Player's Improbable Comeback

Going into the final round of the 1978 Masters, Hubert Green was in the driver's seat with a three-shot lead. Perhaps his greatest threat was Tom Watson, the defending champion, who was tied for second at three behind. No one was paying any attention to Gary Player. The two-time Masters champion, then forty-two, was at 213, seven strokes behind.

Well ahead of the leaders, Player shot a fine 34 on the outward nine—but it was still not enough to get into serious contention. But now Gary really got on a roll. The birdies kept coming throughout the back nine, and Player finally faced a twenty-footer for birdie on hole 18 that would give him a 30 on the back nine and a 64 for the round. After much study, the South African stroked the ball right in the middle, to take a one-stroke lead. He gave a characteristic pump of his clenched right fist. But now Green, who had struggled all day but had remained at or near the top, hit a tremendous approach to the 18th flag, leaving it just three feet away. The birdie would tie him with

Player and force a playoff. Shocking almost every spectator on the premises, Green missed it on the low side, and Gary Player emerged with a most improbable third green jacket.

1986: Nicklaus Wins a Sixth

By 1986, a number of players had surpassed Jack Nicklaus, who was now forty-six years old. Tom Watson and Seve Ballesteros had each taken two Masters titles since Nicklaus's last win, in 1975, and Nicklaus had done nothing early in that season to indicate that he could again contend. At least one sportswriter stated in print that Nicklaus was washed up.

The first round seemed to confirm this prediction. Nicklaus shot a two-over-par 74, but he was encouraged because he had not holed any putts. His rounds improved to 71 and 69 the next two days, but entering the last day he still trailed Greg Norman by five strokes, Seve Ballesteros and Nick Price by three, and Tom Watson and Tom Kite by two. The consensus at the time among the press: there were too many great players on the Augusta course for the aging Nicklaus to catch and pass them all.

Eight holes into the round, it appeared that Nicklaus was indeed a non-factor. At that point he stood even par on his round and had dropped six shots behind. He finally got a spark when he birdied the 9th hole to turn in 35. Birdies at the difficult 10th and 11th holes put Jack in the race. Another birdie at number 13 only offset a bogey 4 at the ticklish 12th, and he still trailed by some three shots.

On the fairway at the par-5 15th hole, Jack asked his son and caddy, Jack Jr., "How far would a three go here?" Jack

Sr. meant an eagle 3, not a three-iron. Jackie replied, "A long way." Nicklaus selected a four-iron and fired a laser right at the flag. It landed near the hole and stopped thirteen feet past. When Nicklaus holed it, perhaps the loudest roar in Augusta National's storied history erupted.

On to hole 16. There, Nicklaus's tee shot landed at the top of the slope to the right of and slightly past the flag, then slowly trickled down, nearly going in for an ace before stopping three feet on the other side. Nicklaus holed his birdie putt, and the gallery erupted. Still, the chances for three others behind—Norman, Kite, and Ballesteros—looked good.

On hole 17, two fine shots by Nicklaus left him with some fourteen feet for birdie, downhill and slightly left to right. His immense concentration firmly intact, the Golden Bear holed the tough putt. The lead, incredibly, was his.

With the 18th hole playing tough with the final-day pin uncharacteristically on the back level, Nicklaus hit the lower level with his approach, then carefully two-putted for a 30 on the back nine, a 65 for the round, and a nine-under-par 279 total. Then, he waited.

When this game is under discussion, it is rarely mentioned that Nicklaus—who undoubtedly played with amazing heart and skill over the final ten holes—also cashed in while all the other contenders either ran into bad luck or made key misplayed shots on the closing holes. Ballesteros, facing a fairly straightforward four-iron second shot to the par-5 15th hole, hit the ball into a pond left of the fairway, bogeyed this near-gimme birdie hole, and made one additional bogey coming in, to finish two back.

Greg Norman, on the 18th fairway, was tied with Nicklaus. From there, he blocked his four-iron way right of the green, and bogeyed to lose by one. And Tom Kite, who saw his twelve-foot birdie attempt to tie Nicklaus on hole 18 graze the top lip, still says to this day that he does not know how the putt missed.

Jack Nicklaus had won his sixth Masters, in what was perhaps the most exciting and emotional victory in the history of golf.

1987: Mize's Miracle Shot

The final round of the 1987 Masters was shaping up as a thriller. The leader board saw Ben Crenshaw with the narrowest of leads over the likes of Greg Norman, Seve Ballesteros, and Bernhard Langer. Few took note of Larry Mize, an Augusta native, who was also in the hunt, two back. As a teenager, Mize had worked at the Masters as a scorekeeper on the scoreboard at the 3rd green, and he dreamed of one day playing in the Masters. In fact, he had stubbornly refused opportunities to play Augusta National until he had qualified to play in the Masters.

When the final seventy-two-hole tallies were in the books, Mize was in a tie with Seve Ballesteros and Greg Norman at three-under-par 285. Mize might have been the sentimental favorite, but everyone expected either Ballesteros or Norman to prevail in the sudden-death playoff.

Norman and Mize each scored par on the first playoff hole, the difficult 10th. Ballesteros was eliminated when he three-putted the green. At the par-4 11th hole, Mize was away after the tee shots. He steered his second shot carefully away from the water guarding the left side of the green—much too carefully. His shot finished well right of the green, about forty-five yards from the flag. When Norman's second shot found the green, about forty feet away, Norman held a large advantage.

Mize's pitch would require the delicacy and steady hand of a brain surgeon. Once the ball reached the green, it would slide slightly downhill on the glassy putting surface, with the water right behind the pin, which was toward the back-left. Mize decided that a shot lofted onto the green probably wouldn't stop. Instead he chose to play a low pitch-and-run, landing the ball short of the green and letting it release. Under intense pressure, Mize struck the shot crisply. Then he and Norman watched for what seemed like an eternity as the ball climbed onto the green, then crept slowly but surely down the sloping green, holding a true line until it finally rapped against the flagstick and dropped in the hole. At this point, Mize made a mighty leap skyward, both arms upraised. The crestfallen Norman gave his long putt a chance, but it was too much to ask to expect him to sink his ball after such an amazing body blow. Longshot Larry Mize donned the green jacket.

1996: Faldo's Fabulous Final Round

After more than a decade filled with near-misses, 1996 appeared, finally, to be Greg Norman's year. After three rounds he had built a commanding six-stroke lead over his nearest pursuer, two-time winner Nick Faldo. The way Norman was playing, it seemed that it would take a course-record round by Faldo, or anyone else, to catch him.

Famous Waterloos at Augusta

There are no water hazards on the first ten holes at Augusta National. But after this point, the Masters competitor must traverse or carry water on five of the next six holes. So it's not surprising that these treacherous hazards, which meander through most of the back nine holes, have figured into the winning equation (or, more often, the losing equation) on several occasions.

Probably the most famous Waterloo occurred in 1954. That year, Billy Joe Patton, a popular amateur North Carolina golfer, had put on a spectacular charge on the front nine. He aced the par-3 6th hole, then followed up with birdies at the 8th and 9th to wrest the lead from the legends Sam Snead and Ben Hogan. After just a fair drive at the tempting par-5 13th hole, Patton was undecided on whether or not to lay up. With fans in his large gallery encouraging him to gamble, Patton decided he couldn't let them down. Unfortunately, he proceeded to dunk his fairway wood shot into the creek fronting the green. After this, a poor fourth shot led to a double-bogey 7.

continued on next page

Round four started innocently enough, but as the front nine progressed, Norman lost a stroke here and there, and Faldo started picking up the pace. The huge crowd was murmuring now. Still, most figured that Norman was too great a player not to right himself and still win the tournament. But Norman kept making errors, while Faldo was turning in a craftsman-like, error-free performance. A brilliant five-wood shot to the par-5 13th hole and the ensuing birdie pretty much stamped the event, amazingly, as Faldo's. By the end, he had carded a fabulous five-under 67 against Norman's shocking 78, and had not only won, but had won easily.

Still, Patton was very much alive going to the par-5 15th hole, where he again opted to go for the carry over the pond to the green. Again Patton splashed his ball and this time made a 6. He ultimately shot a 71 despite these two gaffes, but he finished one stroke behind Snead and Hogan. Just a bogey and a par on these two holes would have made Billy Joe Patton the only amateur to win the Masters.

There is an often-overlooked corollary to Patton's plight in 1954. Right after Patton made his 7 at the 13th hole, Ben Hogan stood in the fairway at the 11th. Hogan always planned to steer well clear of the pond guarding the front-left of that green. At this point in time, Hogan knew that Patton had taken the lead—but he did not know that Patton had just taken a 7 two holes ahead. It is quite likely that Hogan aimed for the green rather than just to the right of it, thinking he needed to give himself a birdie putt. Hogan pulled the shot slightly, and his shot, too, ended up wet. In the end Hogan and Snead tied, but Snead won the playoff the next day, 70 to 71.

continued on next page

1997: Tiger Woods's Smashing Arrival

Even before he turned professional, in 1996, Tiger Woods had shown such enormous talent that it was assumed he would win the Masters not once but many times. No less an authority than Jack Nicklaus stated that Woods could very possibly win ten Masters. Woods, as a three-time U.S. Amateur champion, had already competed at Augusta National. In his first try, in 1995, while still an underclassman in college, Woods shot 72-72-77-72 for a five over par total of 293. Although he had shown amazing power and promise—for example, he had reached the par-5 15th hole with a driver and a pitching wedge—he had not solved all of the great course's subtle challenges, either with his short-iron approaches or on the devilish greens themselves.

Fast-forward to 1985. Curtis Strange was among the very top young players on the PGA Tour, and many saw a green jacket in his future. But Strange skied to an opening-round 80. He then fashioned an amazing comeback, shooting 65 in the second round, and 68 in the third. By midway through the final round he had seized the lead and the momentum was apparently all his.

On the 13th hole, Strange, too, had to decide whether to lay up or go for the green on his second shot. He decided that it was too early to start protecting his lead, and went for it, dropped his four-wood shot into the creek, and made a six. Strange put it in the water again on the par-5 15th hole, and both his momentum and his lead were gone. Bernhard Langer took advantage of the opening to don the first of two green jackets.

The next year, 1986, was a wild one at Augusta. A bevy of big names was in the hunt, and up ahead, Jack Nicklaus was making a spirited charge. But on the 15th fairway, Seve Ballesteros, already a two-time winner, held the lead. He also held a four-iron in his hand, apparently a fairly routine second shot to this par-5. But Ballesteros was uncertain, pondering whether he should change clubs and hit a hard five-iron. Ballesteros decided to stick with the four-iron. Shockingly, Ballesteros pulled the shot into water lurking dangerously left, scored bogey, then made another bogey coming in to finish in fourth place, two behind Nicklaus.

continued on next page

Woods was a pro now. And on the breezy first day of the 1997 tournament he was paired with Nick Faldo, the defending champion and a three-time winner. Early on it looked as though Woods wasn't yet up to the challenge. In fact, he carded a four-over-par 40 on the front nine. Perhaps some were starting to wonder, could Woods possibly go the way of luminaries such as Greg Norman, Tom

Perhaps the most heartbreaking Waterloo occurred in 1990. That year, Ray Floyd, at the age of forty-seven, held the 36- and 54-hole leads and was bidding to become the oldest Masters champion ever. In the last round, Floyd desperately tried to stave off Nick Faldo, the defending champ, but the two tied at ten-under-par 278. After pars at the 10th, the first playoff hole, and after a fine drive at hole 11, Floyd decided to go for the flag with his second. He pulled the shot ever so slightly, but that was enough for the ball to land on the bank and fall back into the pond guarding the left side of the green. Faldo was again the winner.

The greatest Waterloo of all, even though it did not involve the loss of the tournament, has to be that of Tom Weiskopf in 1980. During the first round, Weiskopf hit a seven-iron to the devilish par-3 12th hole. The ball came up short, landing on the bank, then dribbled back into Rae's Creek.

Weiskopf dropped well behind the creek. Still the pitch shot from there might have been more difficult than the tee shot, since it required less than a full swing, played off a downhill lie. Whatever the case, Weiskopf proceeded to put four more balls into the creek before finally hitting the green and two-putting—for a 13. That score, incidentally, tied the record for the highest score on a single hole at the Masters.

The next day, Weiskopf hit just two balls into the water on hole 12, and "only" made a quadruple-bogey 7.

Weiskopf, and Johnny Miller, none of whom ever donned the green jacket?

Woods quickly and resoundingly dispatched any such thoughts. He promptly birdied the 10th, 11th, and 12th holes and followed his outgoing score of 40 with a six-under-par 30. Then, in the second and third rounds, he blew away the field with consecutive rounds of 66 and 65, which gave him a nine-shot advantage heading into the final day. Woods played like a sorcerer and a magician rolled into one, stroking in long putts from everywhere and, when he did stray into Augusta National's many stands of tall pines, inventing miraculous hooked or sliced recoveries that most often found the heart of the putting surfaces.

Woods's final round was more like a coronation than a competition. When he holed a four-foot par putt on the 72nd green for a 69, he had not only won by an unheard-of twelve strokes, but his 270 total had shattered the 72-hole Masters scoring record held jointly by Jack Nicklaus and Ray Floyd. And he did all this while becoming the youngest Masters champion ever—he was just twenty-one years, three months, and fourteen days old. The Age of Tiger Woods had officially begun.

2001: The "Tiger" Slam

After Vijay Singh captured the Masters in 2000, Tiger Woods went on a tear that may never again be matched in tournament golf. In June, at world-famous Pebble Beach for that year's U.S. Open, Woods obliterated the field by fifteen strokes and set a new U.S. Open seventy-two-hole scoring record. The next month, at St. Andrews, Scotland, the home of golf, Woods again decimated the field with a record score, winning the British Open by eight shots. It seemed a foregone conclusion that Woods would also handily take the PGA Championship in August, to be played at Valhalla, near Louisville, Kentucky. Woods did win, defeating journeyman Bob May in a three-hole playoff.

Thus, in April of 2001, Woods had a golden opportunity to win his fourth major championship in a row—what some, including Tiger, would regard as a "Grand Slam." Other purists insist that the Grand Slam must be accomplished within a single calendar year, for example, wins at the Masters, the U.S. Open, the British Open, and the PGA (that is the order in which they take place).

Be that as it may, the pressure on Tiger was terrific, but as usual, he responded to the enormous challenge. Masters rookie Chris DiMarco sprinted into the first-round lead and held it after thirty-six holes at nine-under-par 135. But Woods, with rounds of 70 and 66, was right where he wanted to be. By the end of his third-round 68, Tiger was on top of the heap. However, the final round was anything but a cakewalk. Tiger wound up in a duel with two of the game's other brightest young players, Phil Mickelson (who would win the Masters in 2004 and 2006) and David Duval, who started the final round three back. In fact, Duval was the one with the best chance to stop the "Tiger Slam," as it was beginning to be called. Playing just ahead of Woods and Mickelson, Duval reeled off seven birdies (against two bogeys) in the first ten holes, to tie for the lead. Duval and Woods remained tied after Duval recorded his eighth birdie on hole 15. The key hole turned out to be the par-3 16th. There, Duval's seven-iron shot, which he later said he thought would be stiff, instead flew the green. His ensuing bogey gave Tiger the lead once again. Duval then missed great birdie chances on holes 17 and 18, so that Woods came to the final hole needing only a par to win. After a mammoth drive and a flip sand wedge, Woods holed his twenty-foot putt to prevail by two strokes with a sixteen-under-par 272. So great was his concentration that it was only after the final putt dropped that he realized, Woods later said, that "I didn't have any more shots to play; I had won the Masters."

PART

TWO

HEAVEN ON EARTH

John Andrisani

MY WRITING CAREER has allowed me to visit the most beautiful golf destinations in the world, such as Cypress Point Golf Club in California; Pinehurst in North Carolina; Shinnecock Hills, Garden City, and Winged Foot, all in New York; Baltusrol in New Jersey; Fisher's Island, reached by way of a forty-five minute ferry ride from New London, Connecticut; John's Island West, Jupiter Hills, and Lake Nona in Florida; Ireland's Ballybunion, Portmarnock, and Lahinch courses; St. Andrews and Carnoustie in Scotland; Pedrena in Spain; Etretat in France. Yet when I weigh all the factors that combine to constitute a golf course's greatness—most notably its design, condition, and challenging features—not one matches Augusta National.

Writing about golf for a living has also allowed me to meet some very interesting individuals from numerous different worlds, and many of them have shared their personal stories about visiting Augusta National with me. Shortly, I'll pass their adventurous anecdotes on to you, so that you can fully appreciate the wonder of the Augusta National Golf Club, a club that is managed better than any other in the world and features an adjoining championship course to which no adjective can truly do justice.

In 1984, upon hearing the news that I would be allowed to play the Augusta National course as a guest of this fabled club, I froze, anticipating what the day would be like. So did my three fellow guests—the artist Ron Ramsey, who will provide you with his very own Augusta National story later in this book, and two other players who chose to remain anonymous. We were all so anxious that we needed a few drinks to calm our nerves and help us get to sleep on the evening before making our debut.

The following morning I arrived at the pretty and prestigious Augusta National Golf Club, this time not on assignment for *Golf Magazine* but rather to first play the par-3 course, then next the longer actual championship layout the pros had just finished competing on the day before in the Masters Tournament, with Ben Crenshaw walking off with the coveted green jacket.

Because I was now visiting Augusta National purely for pleasure and not as a working journalist, I was better able to take everything in. Walking with my caddy and my fellow golfers, a voice in my head said, "Welcome, you've arrived in golf heaven."

When I played Augusta's short course it measured a mere 950 yards; the shortest holes, numbers 2 and 4, were just 70 yards, and the longest hole, number 8, was 140 yards. Nevertheless it was still very challenging. The course appeared to be cut out of nature and was as colorful as a painting by Henri Matisse. At every tee, the experience of standing and looking toward the green was practically psychedelic. But rather than hearing music by The Doors or Jimmy Hendrix, I heard silence, broken only by "all of nature yelling fore!" to borrow a line from P. G. Wodehouse. Playing the course was reminiscent of taking walks alone as a boy, through the woods on one corner of my Long Island town road with a cornfield at the other end of it. My contented solitude also brought back memories of trout-fishing days when I was young; just me, my rod, reel, bait, creel, and a lovely little stream in a beautiful landscape. Now, as a thirty-four-year-old man, it was me with golf bag, clubs, ball, and nature. The Augusta National experience was so very different from anything I had experienced on any other golf course, and this par-3 "trip" was only a harbinger of things to come. What awaited me was true fairyland: Augusta's eighteen-hole championship course.

After standing where so many golfing greats had stood, and hitting iron shots off the driving range's sharply mowed green grass, then some drives, and finally putts on the billiard-table-like practice greens, I walked with my caddy and golfing companions past the enormous oak tree behind the simple yet elegant white clubhouse to the first tee.

Arriving on the tee, I was more nervous than I ever had been before when standing over a golf ball. It made absolutely no difference that I had just shot a par score of 27 on the par-3 course, or that during my life I had competed in both professional and amateur tournaments and was used to playing under pressure. There's no pressure equal to standing on the first tee of the Augusta National golf course, especially the first time you do it, no matter how good a golfer you are. I was shaking, and if it not for a pep talk from my very experienced caddy, I might have passed out or had a heart attack.

I managed to hit a decent drive down the left side and hit my second shot about a foot off the green. From that spot I chipped the ball to three feet and faced a slight right-to-left breaking putt; seemingly a relatively easy par-putt to hole. That may be true on other courses, but at Augusta National the ball must find the center of the hole to drop in. Fellow golfers, trust me! At Augusta the ball will never fall in a side or back door; it must be dead center, or you're dead.

As you probably guessed, I missed the par-putt. I might add that after four-putting the fifth green—the first time in my life I had done that—I got used to judging the speed and break in Augusta's lightning-fast sloping greens and ended up shooting a fairly good score, even though it was well above my handicap of three.

The toughness of Augusta made me appreciate how good the PGA Tour pros who "go low" during the Masters are. However, as you know from reading chapter 1 and watching the Masters on television, even the very best golfers sometimes fall victim to the devilish demons that lurk in the shadows in God's own golf country called Augusta National.

Whatever hole you play—particularly the par-4 9th, par-3 12th, and the par-5 15th, you must stay focused and choose either to take a risk and be rewarded for hitting the perfect shot or, failing that, pay a very dear price.

If you ever get a chance to play Augusta, while setting up to play a shot don't let yourself get distracted by the beauty of the course's green tees, fairways, and greens, the pure white sand in the bunkers, or the stunningly gorgeous fauna and flora that surround you. Save your sightseeing time for walking to your ball in between shots. The reason is: No other golf course in the world that I have ever played requires you to concentrate as hard on picking the right club and hitting the right shot. At Augusta, if you are just a little bit off, you'll score double bogey or worse. That's a promise.

Playing Augusta's championship course was much more than a walk in a pretty park. The experience was truly religious. I felt so heightened spiritually that every tall pine, pink Azalea bush, and white-flowered dogwood tree on the border of the course seemed saintly, like apostles, and as I stared in awe playing hole by hole, I felt a surge of warm energy run through my body, as I suspect I will when entering the pearly gates of Heaven and standing before God.

The most menacing feature at Augusta, aside from the hilly fairways and undulated greens that play havoc with your ability to score, is Rae's Creek. Believe me, it is a euphemism to call this a hazard, for if you land in it on any hole where it is present, expect to make a big number.

The fact that I did not play well did not upset me in the least, because I realized that learning the art of scoring at Augusta takes "local knowledge," as we golfers say—time to learn the lay of the land. Unfortunately, it's highly likely that I will never again get the chance to test my skills at Augusta. That's okay. ALL my life I'll be thankful to the Augusta National Golf Club for giving me the opportunity to play both of its two courses, tour the famous clubhouse, view its memorabilia (especially a trophy case containing clubs dedicated by past champions), view the Eisenhower Cabin, taste Augusta's wonderful food, including the club's renowned famous peach cobbler, and drink a rum libation called a Fizz prepared by a veteran bartender who probably passed away years ago. I forget the gentleman's name, but not the ingredients and preparation process involved.

Just in case you feel the urge to test out this cocktail at your local 19th hole, here's what's needed and what to do:

Ingredients: one half ounce lemon juice; one half ounce lime juice; one quarter ounce sugar syrup; two ounces of white rum; soda water.

Preparation: Add ingredients to a Martini shaker containing crushed ice, shake vigorously, strain into a tall glass over ice cubes then fill glass with soda water.

John Andrisani is the former senior instruction editor of Golf Magazine *and the author of several best-selling books, including* The Tiger Woods Way.

CHAPTER
3

STAR QUALITY

Nathaniel Crosby

MY LOVE FOR golf was passed on to me from my father, Bing Crosby, who played the game all over the world. In fact, he died on a golf course in Spain.

What he said about golf in his book, *Bing Crosby's Own Story*, really rings true, and is something I think about often.

"I've been told that I'm relaxed and casual," my father wrote. "If I am, I owe a lot of it to golf. Golf has provided relaxation, which has kept my batteries recharged when I put too heavy a load on them. It doesn't matter what my professional or personal problems are, when I step onto the first tee I get a sense of release and escape. When I concentrate for three to three and a half hours on trying to play a good game, the studio, my radio hour, and the fact that the latest oil well I've invested in is spouting water are unimportant."

My father wrote this book in 1953, the same year Ben Hogan won all three major championships he entered, starting with the Masters in April at Augusta National Golf Club. As my father and I both discovered, Augusta is unquestionably one of the finest places in the world to take a few hours away from the hustle and bustle of life and put everything in perspective.

When I won the 1981 U.S. Amateur, one of the perks was receiving an invitation to play Augusta National in practice rounds prior to the 1982 Masters, and to actually compete in this prestigious tournament.

Like all who make their way through Augusta National's main gate, ride down Magnolia Lane, then get to play Augusta's perfectly conditioned pure green championship course—as I did, first when playing three days running prior to the 1982 Masters with club professional Dave Spencer—I was knocked out.

Dad was right to say Augusta has star quality, I thought while playing the course. From tee to green and in between, Augusta took me on an adventure, and though I hit every club in my bag, had to use my imagination to the utmost, and constantly felt the threat of peril from the course's treacherous hazards, I had fun on all eighteen holes. How good a track is Augusta National? Good enough to be grouped with five other courses that are my other number one favorites:

- Cypress Point, on California's Monterey Peninsula. Many golf aficionados rank this as their favorite golf course.
- Pebble Beach, another California gem, with many holes running along the coast of the Pacific Ocean and the main site for my late father's annual "Clambake" golf tournament.
- Shinnecock Hills, an inland links in Southampton, Long Island, that's been the venue for such prestigious events as the U.S. Open Championship and the Walker Cup Matches.
- Pinehurst Number 2, in Pinehurst, North Carolina, an ingeniously creative Donald Ross–designed course, essentially carved out of a pine forest.
- Seminole, in Palm Beach, Florida, like Augusta an extremely private, professionally managed club that features a spectacular, meticulously manicured course.

When the time came to play in the 1982 Masters, I remember vividly an embarrassing yet somewhat humorous incident that occurred on the practice putting green prior to starting the first round—in thirty-eight-degree weather!

Tom Watson, the defending Masters champion, with whom I was paired, walked over, introduced himself, and wished me good luck. While he was still standing next to me, I dropped three golf balls down on the putting green, as golfers usually do and as I had done hundreds of times before. The only thing was that this time they collided with each other upon landing and shot out in three different directions, disrupting all the other players who themselves were working on their putting strokes and getting a feel for the speed of Augusta's superfast greens. Being good sports, they all just laughed it off, while I stood there feeling as if I had been hazed. Considering the importance of the event, it was like a groom dropping the ring at a royal wedding.

Once play began, I was in such awe of Watson and other golf idols who were competing, plus I had spent so much mental energy thinking about where I found myself and the magnitude of the Masters, that my concentration level was not up to par. Consequently, I shot 43 for nine holes, and because of weather delays I had to come back and complete the other nine in the morning.

The fact that I shot an even par score of 36 on that second nine and didn't play well enough in the second round to make the cut is not what I remember most about the second day's play. What I recall vividly is caddies arriving late and some players such as Tom Weiskopf going wild, particularly because back then a player had to bring his own practice balls to hit on the driving range and needed his caddy to retrieve them. In short, everything was at a standstill until the caddies finally made it to the course.

My greatest moment: standing under the huge oak tree located near the clubhouse, in the same spot where my god-father, the former Masters champion Jack Burke, Jr., had stood in 1965; he had had a photograph taken and sent it to me. On it he had written: "Nathaniel, hope to see you here at Augusta one day."

In 1982, I made me and Jackie proud by playing in the

Masters, and that brought joy to my heart, but as I stared out at the beautiful course that my father had so loved and played so often with such golf lovers as Dwight D. Eisenhower, all I could think of was that I hoped Bing was looking down. And that maybe that familiar golf tip, "Keep your head down," has a much deeper meaning.

Nathaniel Crosby, son of the immortal singer and avid golfer Bing Crosby, is famous in his own right. He won the 1981 United States Amateur Championship and played Tour golf before entering golf's business world. The former vice president of sales at Orlimar Golf and president of the Nicklaus Golf Company, Nathaniel is now working on some new ventures that promise to powerfully impact the world of golf.

CHAPTER
4

Absolutely No Admittance

Jay Connolly

THERE ARE SIX of us descending on Atlanta from different parts of the country. This is no ordinary golf junket. It's the first leg of my inaugural visit to Augusta National. We all meet at dinner and our anticipation of the next day dominates the conversation. A great meal amid a collegial setting concludes with team assignments and the mandatory briefing on Augusta protocol. In short, don't screw up and you may be invited back. These, of course, are the same rules for a private audience with the pope at the Vatican. With the teams picked and the bet set, the tour of Atlanta's nightlife begins.

The next morning, a short hop by private jet has us

circling the Augusta National Golf Club at three thousand feet. It's beautiful!

In the blink of the eye, we are in a rental car on our way to the most famous of golf courses.

After driving through the top-security guard-gate and proceeding down Magnolia Lane we set foot on the hallowed grounds of Augusta and are immediately welcomed by our hosts. At first glance I see that Augusta's clubhouse matches the surrounding land and radiates understated excellence. It's everything I expected and more as I tiptoe around keeping up a pretense of calm.

After a short drive to the guest cottages, it's off to the par-3 course to shed the jitters that lurk within last night's cobwebs. For some reason, and I can't remember why, my teammate and I choose to drive our rental car to the "short course," instead of being escorted by our hosts and getting to our destination on foot. Little did I know that we were about to be tested.

It all happens quickly as I take a wrong turn on to a maintenance road and get lost. A serpentine maze ends abruptly at a green gate. Are we in the Land of Oz? Approaching the gate, it magically opens up to civilization and Washington Road, the main drag closest to Augusta. The dance begins.

Too far to back up and running late, I take the gamble. Composing my story on the run, we close rapidly—once again—on the main entrance gate. I remember the sign vividly—terse and unambiguous it reads, "Absolutely No Admittance." Gulp! The guard steps off his post, uniform starched, clipboard in hand. A quick head feint to my navigator, Hanzel, signals who will do all the talking.

I begin my story by explaining how me and my golf

partner had been flushed out the green maintenance gate and tell the guard politely that all we would like to do is reenter the grounds to join our hosts, member's X and Y. After a glimpse at both our sheepish smiles, the guard's eyes shift to a clipboard held in his hands. The decision is quick and courteous. "My clipboard says that all the guests of Mr. X and Mr. Y are on the grounds. Since you're on the grounds, you can't be here." Then the big hammer falls as he dials the clubhouse to page our hosts to vouch for and escort us back on the grounds. We clasp our hands and plead like children, but it's all over now.

I slump down in the seat looking through the steering wheel at the two golf carts traveling our way. Will the torture be slow? Will the end be quick? Our hosts, thankfully, see the humor in our adventure and welcome us back through the Pearly Gates. Our fellow travelers, on the other hand, are not as understanding and the ritual hazing of the freshman begins. After a full measure of penance, I have to whisper to each: "Your name has permanently been scratched for allowing the rookies to violate the escort rule. Have a good round."

Today, as I relive my many rounds at Augusta, laughter has eclipsed embarrassment. And when asked about my first visit, I retort with a wink: "It got better after I choked on Magnolia Lane."

Jay Connolly is the former managing director of Salomon Brothers in New York City. A low-handicap golfer, Connolly is presently the director of Waterville Golf Links in Waterville, Ireland, a fabulous links course redesigned by Tom Fazio, the very same architect who made the most recent changes to Augusta National golf course.

CHAPTER 5

"Vintage" Augusta

James W. Finegan

Philadelphia-area golfers incline to be snooty. Perhaps understandably so. The consensus greatest course in the world, Pine Valley, is here. So is Merion, its East Course inarguably among America's top ten. To say nothing of Aronimink, designed by Donald Ross; Philadelphia Cricket Club, created by A. W. Tillinghast; Philadelphia Country Club, laid out by William Flynn; and Whitemarsh Valley, designed by George C. Thomas. Also handsomely represented are courses by Tom Doak, Tom Fazio, Jack Nicklaus, Robert Trent Jones, Rees Jones, the teams of Bill Coore and Ben Crenshaw, and of Arnold Palmer and Ed Seay, plus other gems by first-rank architects.

Over the decades during which I managed to play most of the American shrines and all of the worthy courses of Britain and Ireland, I somehow never got to Augusta National. What's more, I did not feel deprived. Exposure to it via television, magazines, newspapers, and books provided some knowledge of the golf holes, or, at the very least, of the back nine, that cavalcade of brilliant and tension-rife holes, including half a dozen that are great by even the most rigorous standards.

And then, in the late nineties, I was invited to Augusta to play a round, stay overnight in the clubhouse following that first round, and play the course a second time the following morning. Just the experience of rooming in the charming clubhouse was enough to conjure up a feeling of heavenly delight, yet it was the course that really bowled me over.

The second nine holes were all I was confident they would be. But the revelation for me was the front nine. Was it as good as the back? Is it a great nine? Oh my, yes. The risk-reward element is high; the elevation changes are splendid, particularly on holes 2, 4, 6, and 8; trees frame each hole but never claustrophobically; bunkers—twenty-four in all—are cunningly deployed; and the greens are quintessentially Augusta—big, terrifyingly contoured, full of unnerving pin positions.

Every hole is worthy and at least four are outstanding: the 350-yard 3rd, which the 1992 Masters champion Fred Couples rightly calls "one of the best short par-fours anywhere"; the 455-yard 5th, rising modestly, bending vigorously left, two cavernous pits in the crook of the dogleg at

290 yards, a big knoll in front of the defiantly complex green; the 180-yard 6th hole, a steeply falling shot with a huge pit across the front of the green and a couple of satanic shelves in the rear of it that prompt three- and four-putting; and the 460-yard 9th, downhill to a narrow landing area in the trees, followed by a left turn and a climb to an elevated green that has a drop of more than eight feet from back to front.

So terrific is this first nine, so full of challenge and fascination and diversity and Bernard Darwin's "pleasurable excitement," that we don't even notice the total absence of water. But the second nine will take care of that department. And the entire eighteen, even for a condescending Philadelphian, deserves to be ranked among the five greatest courses in the world. Anything else? The club's wine cellar is flabbergasting. So I feel compelled to tell you the story of how I felt much like the wine connoisseur in Edgar Allen Poe's short story "The Cask of Amontillado" when lured into the cellar.

My host, Phil Harrison, is known to the business world for his expertise in selling insurance, but he is also connected to Augusta as the gentleman who announces the names of the competitors during the Masters every April, when the tournament is played. Phil was given the "job" some sixty years ago, when Bob Jones convinced him that the classy thing to do was to properly introduce each player. Of course, Phil agreed; not only because nobody ever turned down a request by Jones, but because he believed it to be proper protocol.

Upon completion of the round, I was invited to dinner

with Phil and his son. And though I was overwhelmed by the quality of food as well as the impeccable service, my taste buds were reacting most to a variety of wines that seemed to have no equal. The whites and reds were absolutely spectacular. Phil could hardly help but notice my reactions, so he invited over to our table the club's wine steward. After seeing the expression of excitement on my face and hearing the numerous adjectives I used to describe the quality of wine I had already tasted, he invited me to take a tour of the wine cellar—which I had never read about nor heard mentioned by anyone inside or outside the golf business.

After a quick "Yes, of course, I would be honored and delighted to see the cellar," there I was following the steward down a set of somewhat hidden stairs located in the back corner of the dining room. Minutes later I found myself amidst walls and walls of vintage wines—burgundies, Cabernets, clarets, Merlots, champagnes. Connoisseurs can say what they want about such grand cellars, like the one in New York's "21" restaurant. To me, there is little question that Augusta's member-owned wine cellar is the greatest in the country—stocked with only the very best vintages, as is to be expected. After all, nothing is second class at Augusta.

Jim W. Finegan is a member of Pine Valley Golf Club in New Jersey and Philadelphia Country Club in Pennsylvania. Finegan, a renowned author and low-handicap golfer who lives in Villanova, Pennsylvania, is best known for writing A Centennial Tribute to Golf in Philadelphia *and* Pine Valley Golf Club: A Unique Haven of the Game, *as well as his books covering golf in Scotland, Ireland, England, and Wales.*

CHAPTER
6

THE VERDICT

John Andrisani

A FEW YEARS after I was hired to work as instruction editor for *Golf Magazine*, Mike Bryan was drafted from Hollywood, where he was involved with such movies as *The Verdict*, to become our publication's chief feature editor. I found that ironic because when our office moved from 380 Madison Avenue to 2 Park Avenue in New York City, the bar at the Sheraton Park Avenue Hotel, where a classic scene for *The Verdict* was filmed, was located very close by.

I got along with Mike better than anyone else on our staff, admiring him for his clear, cut-and-dried thinking and attention to detail, which was reflected in his wonderfully edited pieces. Frankly, he should be an editor at *The New Yorker*. What's more, because Mike had a passion for golf, had visited many great courses, and was never one to mince words, I looked forward to his return from his first trip to Augusta when I would get to hear his opinions.

Before giving me *The Verdict*, he reminded me of a quote by Augusta's designer, Alister MacKenzie: "The chief object of every golf architect or greens-keeper worth his salt is to imitate the beauties of nature so closely as to make his work indistinguishable from nature itself."

Mike then told me essentially what he later wrote about the Augusta National golf course in his book about golf, *Dogleg Madness*.

No golf course I had ever seen was remotely as beautiful. That's outrageous hyperbole, but you wouldn't have to play golf to agree that Augusta National in the right conditions is one of the prettiest spots on earth. The shapes of the greens and the sculpting of the bunkers filled with bright sand and their integration into the broader landscape of fairways and vistas are the equivalent in landscape of one of Henry Moore's heavy, fecund sculptures. Each is modern art.

Mike Bryan worked as the story editor for movie producers Richard Zanuck and David Brown, was senior features editor at Golf Magazine, *and is a free-lance writer best known for collaborating on* If at First *with former National League first baseman Keith Hernandez, and, most recently,* The Storm: What Went Wrong During Hurricane Katrina—The Inside Story from One Louisiana Scientist, *with Ivor van Heerden.*

CHAPTER
7

THE EIGHTH WONDER OF THE WORLD

John Andrisani

"CHI CHI" RODRIGUEZ is one golfer who should have won the Masters, and it is odd that he never did. The reasons he could have gotten a green jacket: he hits a controlled power-draw off the tee, ideal for curving the ball around Augusta's dogleg-left holes, is a shot-making virtuoso, a short game wizard, and an excellent course manager.

I wrote the book *101 Supershots* with Chi Chi in 1990, worked with him on several instruction articles while a senior editor of *Golf Magazine*, chatted with him over lunch, and played golf with him. Finally, one day, the subject of the Masters Tournament came up, and I asked him to tell me his first impressions of the Augusta National course and to cite the chief reason why he had never won the green jacket. I know Chi Chi as an engaging conversationalist, but nevertheless I was surprised by his answer.

"Augusta National golf course is so extraordinarily beautiful that I consider it the Eighth Wonder of the World, and when I first played it I found myself thanking God just to be alive," said Chi Chi.

"In other words, John, Augusta affected me so much spiritually and made me feel so good that, in looking back, maybe I lost a little bit of the competitive edge I needed to win.

"To win the Masters, you must concentrate harder than when playing any other course, because there is no margin for error. Each shot must not only be planned out correctly, it must be executed precisely—or else! At Augusta, in such beautiful surroundings, I could not help letting my mind wander to thoughts of how fortunate I was just to be playing the golf course and that winning golf tournaments is not the most important thing in life. Those same thoughts about the most important things in life spring to mind when I look at the beautiful face of an underprivileged child."

Juan "Chi Chi" Rodriguez is a veteran tour professional, having won eight times on the PGA Tour and twenty-two times on the Senior PGA Tour (Champions Tour). Chi Chi is also known for his generous charity work, raising millions of dollars to help the underprivileged.

CHAPTER
8

"BYE-BYE" BALL

Larry Harrison

IN 1986, TWO weeks before the Masters Tournament, I finally realized my dream of visiting Augusta, Georgia, to play the Augusta National golf course—America's Mecca of golf—with Rocco Mediate, a professional golfer and PGA Tour player whom I was sponsoring at the time, and his teacher, Rick Smith.

For all of us, this was our first trip to Augusta, venue of the Masters, and as it was so close to the start of the tournament, we knew the course would be in even finer condition than normal. All of us, Rocco included, were anxious to take everything in and savor every single moment. I started doing that the second we entered Augusta's guarded gate and drove down the famous Magnolia Lane toward the clubhouse.

What first struck my eyes was the Augusta clubhouse; though much smaller than I imagined, it carried an unparalleled degree of historical presence, and was to me as a golfer what the White House is to me as an American. And what lay behind it was truly magnificent: the penetrating green of the course, a sea of green tees, fairways, and putting surfaces that were as tightly woven as a Persian carpet.

Once on the course itself I felt the history of past Masters contests run through my blood with every step, and I quickly discovered how tough the course is to shoot a low score on. Because of the severe undulations in the greens, putting is very difficult, although it helps to follow the advice of Augusta's caddies: All putts break toward Rae's Creek. Chip shots, particularly on hole 14, also test your short-game skills to the ultimate. You must choose the right club and be precise with your judgment of direction and speed, or else you will never hit the ball close to the hole. In fact, you may even hit the green with a chip shot and watch the ball roll back to your feet or over the green, the way I did in front of the great Jack Nicklaus. To this day, I'll never forget Jack saying, "Bye-Bye," as soon as the ball left my club.

If you should ever be invited to visit Augusta, don't expect to find it to be a sleepy town, as I did. Augusta, Georgia, is anything but. You'll know what I mean when you drive down Washington Road on your way to the club and pass blocks and blocks of shops and businesses. My advice: Close your eyes until a friend taps you on the shoulder and says, "We've arrived."

Once you find yourself driving down Magnolia Lane, I guarantee you won't be able to shut your eyes again as long as you are on the grounds of the Augusta National Golf Club. Furthermore, for years and years after your visit, images of Augusta will flash through your mind like segments of your favorite movie. Enjoy the show!

Larry Harrison is a New Jersey based beer-business entrepreneur for Anheuser-Busch and Heineken, the chairman of the Shop-Rite LPGA Classic, three-handicap golfer, and a member of several prestigious country clubs.

CHAPTER
9

HAMMING IT UP AT AUGUSTA

Ron Ramsey

IN 1984, WHEN I got word that I was likely to be a guest
of the Augusta National Golf Club and play the course for
the very first time on the Monday after the Masters, I prac-
ticed at home during very cold March weather. Wanting to
perfect my swing so that I was less likely to choke on the
first tee at Augusta and top my opening tee shot, I hit only
drives during my practice sessions.

Fortunately, when the day arrived, the arrangements
were such that our group was to play the par-3 course first,
in order to acclimatize ourselves for playing Augusta's "real
course," which would be equivalent to standing on the

diamond at Yankee Stadium, in uniform, and being pitched to by a big league ballplayer.

Surprisingly, I played the par-3 course very well, so well that on the 115-yard 9th hole, I hit a tee-shot one foot from the hole. Standing over the putt, it suddenly hit me that I was playing at Augusta, and since the putt was for quite a bit of money, I got a taste of how much pressure the pros experience when standing over a breaking putt, even a tap-in like the one I was facing. Before I tell you what happened, I must inform you that the greens are so fast that I can well understand why Tiger Woods reportedly prepared for his first Masters by practicing putting on Stanford University's gymnasium floor. If ever I were to be invited back to Augusta, I would practice putts in my bathtub.

I missed the putt, with the ball not even shaving the hole. In fact, because the greens are so fast I actually rolled the ball by the hole and faced an even longer putt than the first one. This time, however, I stroked the ball into the center of the cup for par, which allowed my partner, John Andrisani, and me to win the match, though not win as big a bet as we could have.

Now warmed up, I got the chance to play the same course the pros had just played. It was the Monday after the Sunday when Ben Crenshaw had won his first Masters.

My driving practice paid off, since I hit a super drive off the 1st tee. All the same, the Augusta course sure got the best of me. Augusta looks so easy, but it is the hardest course in the world, owing largely to the hilly fairways and undulating lightning-fast greens. Chipping and putting are particularly hellish.

As spectacular as the Augusta course is, two things stand out in my memory that have nothing to do with the wonderful eighteen holes:

1. The ham sandwiches wrapped in Augusta-green paper are delicious, and that's coming from a guy who sometimes visits New York delicatessens.
2. The coolest thing is to stand under the giant oak tree right next to the clubhouse, knowing that during the Masters this is the ultimate gathering place for players and guests, who are all so happy to be part of the scene.

So, more than anything else, it's the tradition of this classiest of golf clubs that stand out in my mind. My only regret: I failed to bring my sketch pad; oh how I would love to have painted that oak tree and the folks under it, or a still life of a table with an Augusta-green tablecloth with a ham sandwich atop it. Still, I guess I will have to be satisfied that I have vividly colorful scenes painted for all time in my mind.

Ron Ramsey is a renowned illustrator whose work has appeared in leading publications, most notably the Saturday Evening Post *and* Golf Magazine. *A member of the Society of Illustrators in New York City and the Siwanoy Country Club in Bronxville, New York, Ramsey, a single-digit player, is best known for his portraits of such golfing greats as Ben Hogan, Masters chamption. He is presently the art director for* Northeast Golf.

CHAPTER
10

INSIDE THE ROPES

Greg Hood

IN 1980, I was the PGA Tour manager for the Ben Hogan Company. That same year I made my first trip to Augusta National to meet at the golf course with our company's professional staff. I felt as if I was actually going to play in the Masters Tournament, so I could not wait to arrive at the gates to Magnolia Lane and judge for myself the greatness of the course. I was so excited and nervous that I actually had butterflies in my stomach.

From the moment I drove down the most memorable lane in all of golf, I actually admit to having a surreal experience.

On first seeing the course, in all its green glory and its amazingly impressive serenity, I truly felt as though I was in

Heaven, particularly after meeting with players I knew and seeing expressions on their faces I had never before witnessed. At other Tour events, I was used to a sort of casual party atmosphere. At Augusta, it was all business, with top golf professionals caught up in their own special solitary thoughts.

Although my first wonderful experience at Augusta is etched in my mind forever, so, too, is a visit I made later, in 1985. That year I got to walk the entire course (inside the ropes, rather than outside the ropes as I had had to do five years earlier) during a practice round and eavesdrop on my host, the PGA Tour player Mac O'Grady and the two-time Masters champion Severiano Ballesteros, who was teaching Mac how to approach the course. Seve was imparting to Mac local knowledge on where and where not to hit the ball off the tee and on the green and also how to look at the tips of trees to determine the "hidden" winds that you do not feel at ground level.

I will be forever grateful to Mac for inviting me to be a guest of his because even though I did not play the course, from up close I really got a good look at how dramatically hilly the fairways are and how difficult the pin positions can be on Augusta's notorious undulated greens.

It was, of course, also wonderful to watch Seve in action, and although Mac did not perform well in that year's Masters, I can only hope that someday he will have the opportunity to return, even if he's a guest of a member rather than a competing player, and prove to himself that he can beat what Greg Norman calls "The tough old gal."

Greg Hood is a California-based golf consultant and the former personal assistant to the legendary golfer and two-time Masters winner Ben Hogan.

DON'T ALWAYS GRIP IT AND RIP IT AT AUGUSTA

John Andrisani

THE PGA TOUR pro John Daly loves Augusta National, and, make no mistake, his phenomenal power and his exceptional short-game touch—which is rarely, if ever, mentioned by television golf commentators—make him anything but a long shot to win a Masters title.

There's not one phony streak in John Daly. What's more, he doesn't keep anything close to his vest and he's always nice to members of the press, opening up as freely as he lets his driver rip on the course, hitting one booming 300-yard tee shot after another.

Daly has yet to win the Masters, but he finished first in

the 1991 PGA and the 1995 British Open, which is not surprising considering his two chief shot-making attributes: power and touch.

Daly played in his first Masters in 1992, eventually finishing in nineteenth place. That was actually a good showing, because learning where the best places are to land the ball off the tee and on the green and how putts break takes years of experience. That's what Daly told me in 1992, when we worked on the book *Grip It and Rip It!*

I talked to Daly again after he finished third in the Masters in 1993 and he laughed when I said, "John, I guess you learned a lot about local knowledge since you first played."

He replied, "Yeah, I really think I can win at Augusta, provided I discipline myself not to let the driver rip so often on par-four and par-five holes, and work more on controlling the speed of my putts."

We talked some more about Augusta National and Daly made a point of saying it was the best-conditioned course in the world.

I found it particularly amusing when I asked him whether there was anything he would change and he said jokingly: "Yeah, I wish there were ashtrays around the course for me to put out my butts."

John Daly, one of golf's most popular players, is the author of the hot new book, My Life in and out of the Rough: The Truth Behind All That Bull**** You Think You Know About Me.

THERE'S NOTHING LIKE CADDY DAY

Tripp Bowden

MY FIRST MEMORY of Augusta was a photograph—a slide my dad used for a slide show and talk he put together for the Georgia Surgical Society. I was twelve years old and knew as much about golf as I did about cricket.

The slide carousel whirred and stopped on a breathtaking wintertime photo of Augusta's treacherous 12th hole, an unforgiving par-3 where the wind usually swirls and demands that the golfer hit a 155-yard shot over Rae's Creek to an extra-narrow green. A rare southern snowfall had left everything in the photo white—everything but the green, that is, for it is heated and cooled year-round by a clever contraption hidden in a pump house to the left of the pond on hole 11.

Me, the punk kid who had to yet break 100 and hadn't made his eighth-grade golf team (just like Michael Jordon, but that's where the comparison ends), even though I had made a hole-in-one, would soon—starting in 1983—play Augusta National many times as a guest of the pro's son during what was known as Closing Week. During Closing Week's seven days there were tee times every seven minutes, and tournament bigwigs, scorekeepers, grounds crew, staff, and even caddies got their big chance to put a peg in the ground and experience the sacred grounds of Augusta National.

What first impressed me was how lush yet flat to the ground the grass was, and soft; walking on it was like walking on a big green cloud. The tee boxes were easily as fast as those of most greens I had played (I remember putting on them), and the air smelled of tradition and reverence. And the course was quiet, so incredibly quiet. All those people milling about, and I don't remember hearing a single voice.

Fast-forward to 1989. I was the proud owner of a B.A. degree, having majored in English and minored in philosophy and psychology. I was either going to teach or stare out the window. But luck shone on me once again and the caddy master of Augusta, a very close friend of my father's, took me under his wing and gave me a job. I was the only full-time white caddy at Augusta National. I felt like the luckiest man alive. Looking back, I believe I was.

I learned so much about an Augusta National caddy, and very little of it did I learn on my own. I was fortunate enough to have many teachers, every one of them with their own special insight into the brotherhood of caddying, too many to list here. But here is one I must share: Sidney Brown preached, "You don't read Augusta's greens, you remember them."

Caddies were allowed to play Augusta just once a year, the final day of Closing Week. There is nothing in the world quite like Caddy Day at Augusta National, when we had free run of those hallowed grounds, except for the club-house. Tee off at sunrise with four carts in your foursome as you try to break the record for most holes played in one day (105, if memory serves). Fish Ike's Pond with your new friends, fellow caddies who taught you to love "looping" or carrying the golf bag side of the game as much as golf itself. Sit on the verandah just like a member, drinking cold draft beer and smoking Kool cigarettes while telling stories about playing Augusta for the first time.

As strange as this may sound, my perspective on playing Augusta National as a caddy seemed almost secondary to getting to really know the course. It was like finally getting to talk to a beautiful woman whom you know only because she walks by your office every day. On Caddy Day you get to learn that beautiful woman's name, her likes and dislikes, her hopes and dreams, thoughts and wishes. And she learns yours. And if only for that day, she belongs to you.

Fast-forward to 1994 and see me sitting in a barber's chair in Atlanta, getting my hair cut. My phone rings and normally I would hit the "No thanks, I'm busy" button, but I see it's my dad and I answer. He rarely calls, so it must be important. I put the phone to my ear.

"Want to play Augusta tomorrow?"

I drop the phone—literally. I have never played Augusta as a guest of a member. I'm having trouble catching my breath. Less than twenty-four hours and a short drive from Atlanta later, I'm driving through the front gate and down Magnolia Lane. But today I'm not arriving to caddy.

Ten minutes later I arrive on the practice tee—with my own caddy! I admit it felt odd to be on the other side of the white jump suits caddies wear at Augusta.

Soon after warming up, I find myself standing on the first tee, finding it hard to believe I am really ready to start playing Augusta National as a member's guest. My hands shake so badly I worry that I will not be able to tee up my golf ball. My mind races with everything that defines me as a golfer. I can't believe I was once a ten-year-old kid who took his Walter Hagen junior set of clubs into the street and beat them like drumsticks, angry because my dad would rather watch stupid golf than kick a soccer ball. Then, two years later, I fell in love with Augusta National during a Monday practice round, eating a pork chop sandwich from the caddy house while watching the U.S. Open champion Jerry Pate stripe drive after drive into a net that seemed miles away. Suddenly the game of golf was no longer stupid but the most wonderful thing in the world. All these remembrances of things past flash through my brain as I prepare to play my first "official" shot.

I manage to steady my ball on the tee and quickly snap-hook my drive behind one of the tallest trees at Augusta. When I reach my ball it is resting against the trunk. My caddy looks at me and says, "Now what?" I'll let you guess what my response was. Thankfully, I manage to score bogey and go on to play a fairly decent round of golf.

A lot of water has washed under the bridge since that day, and my life is very different and so are my perspectives. I hope this won't jeopardize my chances of ever getting invited back, but I have to be honest: There is nothing quite like Caddy Day. Playing Augusta as the guest of a member doesn't quite stack up.

Tripp Bowden is director of Behind The Curtain Creative Services, Inc., in Atlanta, Georgia, and the author of a novel, Greyhound Jesus and the Perpetual Care Fund.

CHAPTER
13

COVERED IN GREEN

John Andrisani

CLAUDE "BUTCH" HARMON, JR., is best known for being the longtime instructor of the four-time Masters champion Tiger Woods. What few know is that Butch is the son of Claude Harmon, Sr., one of the game's best instructors ever, who helped golfers improve at two famous clubs: Winged Foot in New York and Seminole in Florida. Harmon Senior also just so happened to win the 1948 Masters.

I'm fortunate to have played golf with Butch at my former club, Lake Nona, in Orlando, Florida, as well as to work with him on magazine articles for *Golf Magazine* and two books, *The Four Cornerstones of Winning Golf* and *Butch Harmon's Playing Lessons*.

It was during the collaboration process of the first book, still a best-seller, that I really took the opportunity to pick Butch's brain.

It was natural for Butch to tell me he had a special affection for Augusta National, considering his father had won the Masters Tournament. The thing is, Butch was only four years old back then, so he did not remember much about the course, but he did have these things to say.

"I was too young to remember much at the time of my father's victory. I was staying in Augusta, Georgia, where the Masters is played every year, with my mom and dad. Dad came in late after a night of celebration. According to my mom, when he returned "home" he covered me with a green jacket given to him as the Masters winner. This warm gesture had made perfect sense, for dad always shared everything with me. Not many sons can say they had a Masters green jacket draped over them during their lifetime!

"Over the years I asked my dad, hundreds of times, about his long-shot victory, and he was always modest about the way he played, not really ever bragging about how during the final round he clinched the tournament by going birdie, birdie, and eagle on holes 6, 7, and 8. He also was generous in giving Craig Wood, his former boss at Winged Foot, credit. Wood had won the 1941 Masters and prior to the start of the 1948 Masters, shared his local knowledge about Augusta National with Dad, telling him which shots to practice. Consequently, Dad was ready for battle.

"Dad also told me that, although Augusta looks wide open and the greens huge, you have to hit drives in the ideal landing area to set up an aggressive approach shot into the green and also land the ball on a precise spot in order to have any chance of scoring birdie. According to Dad, Wood helped him with local knowledge, but also playing Winged Foot's West course and Seminole—two courses featuring rolling terrain, tree-lined fairways, and undulated greens of sundry shapes and sizes—helped his eyes prepare for the similar features of Augusta National and thus helped him to hit the right shots at the right time."

Claude "Butch" Harmon, Jr., formely the coach of Tiger Woods, has been ranked the number one teacher in America by Golf Digest, *and now instructs some of the PGA Tour's best players, including Adam Scott.*

CHAPTER
14

THE SECRET WEAPON

John Andrisani

IN 1995, I collaborated with the golf pro Craig Stadler to write *I Am the Walrus: Confessions and Tips from a Blue-Collar Golfer.*

While writing this offbeat book, I had the chance to talk with Craig about the total game, on the golf course and off it, over a few beers. Craig has always been known as a player who lets out his emotions, yet still is a very intelligent player who rarely makes an unforced error during an eighteen-hole round, no matter how furious he gets.

When I asked Craig about the pressure of being in the hunt in day 4 of the Masters, he admitted that the stretch of back-nine holes called Amen Corner is critical, because one missed shot can lead to disaster and cost you victory. I had heard other players, both winners and losers, say the same thing. But I never heard one tell me something else Craig told me.

"To win at Augusta, you need *one* secret weapon," said Craig. "For me it's the sand wedge. I play just about every single short-game shot with this club. For others it may be the putter, driver—whatever, you need one club you can depend on during the Masters to boost your confidence and get the job done for you."

Having worked with Craig on the aforementioned book as well as magazine articles for *Golf Magazine*, I can assure you that he truly is a wedge wizard. My recommendation: should you ever be fortunate enough to play Augusta National, know how to work the ball with your sand wedge, and follow these two bits of advice Craig gave me:

1. To develop a variety of shots, try different setups and swings.
2. When practicing, note how the ball reacts in the air and on the ground relative to the changes made in your setup and swing. The more shots you learn, the lower scores you will shoot.

Craig is a great improviser with the sand wedge, and able to hit a variety of shots, his favorite being a high, soft-landing lob over a bunker to a tight pin, especially one out of the rough.

On the basis of tips from Craig, here's how to play

this shot that you'll need at Augusta or at your home course.

- Provided you have a cushion of grass under the ball, so that you can get the leading edge of your wedge underneath the ball, the secret is to play this shot like a bunker shot from sand.
- In setting up, open your stance and the club face of your wedge. The higher and softer the shot you need, the more open both should be.
- Employ a compact backswing, allowing your right wrist to hinge freely.
- On the downswing, let your right wrist unhinge so that you can more easily slap the grass just behind the ball, much as you would the sand when playing a bunker shot. Impact will inevitably be muffled somewhat, so make sure to follow through fully to encourage ample acceleration in the hitting area.
- If the swing is executed correctly, the ball will fly high and drop softly on the green; just the type of shot you want to hit on superfast super-sloped greens like the ones at Augusta National.

Craig Stadler, nicknamed "The Walrus," won the 1982 Masters and now plays the Champions Tour, where he continues to show his total-game prowess.

CHAPTER
15

Seve at Home at Augusta National

John Andrisani

SEVERIANO BALLESTEROS, NICKNAMED Seve, is a former number one world-ranked golf professional and as a two-time Masters winner has been presented with two green jackets.

In 1984 I traveled to Severiano Ballesteros's hometown, Pedrena, in northern Spain, to work on a series of golf-instructional articles for *Golf Magazine*. While there I got to play his home course, Real Club de Golf de Pedrena, the same one he has played since as a young boy when he had dreams of becoming the number one golfer in the world. Later, in 1986, I traveled to Alicante, Spain, to actually play with Seve at the La Manga Golf Club, at which time he showed me how to hit a variety of inventive shots he had learned as a boy from his uncle, Ramón Sota, a fine player in his own right, and by experimenting with different grips, stances, and swings when practicing.

During my trips to *España* we spent hours talking on and off the golf course, so it was inevitable that the subject of the Masters and the Augusta National Golf Club would come up. After all, Seve had already won two Masters titles, in 1980 and 1983.

When I mentioned Augusta, Seve told me the very same thing he had told the golf writer Dudley Doust when they collaborated on the book *Seve: The Young Champion*. From the time Seve first set foot on the Augusta National course, in 1977, he said, he felt at home because the layout and scenery was similar to the lush, rolling Pedrena course, also lined with pine trees, which he had played hundreds of times.

"When I saw Augusta, it gave me a very familiar feeling," said Seve. "These were my trees, my color of green, and I told myself I would win this tournament one day."

Seve finished in thirty-third place in 1977; the following year he played the final round with the eventual winner, Gary Player, who scored seven birdies over the last ten holes. In 1978, Seve finished in seventeenth place, and in 1979, in the twelfth spot.

Seve's first win came in 1980, when he shot a phenomenal seventy-two-hole score of 275, and then in 1983 won again, shooting 280 over four days of competition. Seve made a point of telling me that he won these tournaments for his country, where he is a hero, and for Uncle Ramón, who had played in six Masters but had never won.

When I asked Seve why he loved Augusta so much, he told me that it is a course that made him feel as if he were in a ring with a bull.

"To win the battle—the Masters—you must concentrate intently and never let your guard down, be cautiously aggressive and play the percentages since a well-planned somewhat risky shot can earn you birdie or eagle, while a silly shot can cost you double bogey or worse," said Seve. "You must also remain patient, stay level-headed, so as not to get too high or low and lose your intensity, remain confident from start to finish, and mentally block out the sounds of the gallery so that it's just you and the course in a bubble."

While in Spain on another trip years earlier, a Spanish woman told me that the only real men left in the world are matadors. If I could see that woman today, I'd tell her that the only real men left in the world are those who can withstand the pressure of the last nine holes of the Masters and emerge the winner, as Seve did twice in the course of his illustrious career. These are men who possess more courage than the bullfighter, because they must win their battle using a golf club rather than a sword, against an adversary who is much tougher and less vulnerable than a bull trapped in a ring.

Severiano Ballesteros is best known for his 1980 and 1983 Masters wins, and for his three British Open victories, in 1979, 1984, and 1988.

CHAPTER
16

Surprise, Surprise

Jim Hardy

Before playing Augusta National, my perceptions were that you had to hit the ball high, that there was a great premium on long driving, and that the putting element was overly emphasized. Chances are that you, too, think that Augusta is a bomber's paradise with plenty of room to drive the ball and little penalty for off-line shots. Also, that a long hitter off the tee has a huge advantage on the par-5 holes, particularly if he can carry the ball onto down slopes in the fairways. Furthermore, that high, soft-landing second shots to pins located just beyond false fronts reward the high-ball hitter with makeable birdie efforts. (The golfing legend Lee

Trevino had often said that his low-ball flight was not suited for Augusta. My perceptions before I played Augusta were that he was right.)

When it came to my thoughts on putting, the television announcers have always emphasized the slopes and contours on the greens. Although not well seen on the screen, I could imagine how the green's expansive rolls, ridges, hollows, and bumps would make putting very difficult. I figured, if ever I got the chance to play Augusta National and if any part of my short game, particularly putting, was off, I would be humbled unmercifully.

I have always been aware of the history and lore of Augusta National. All the great players of the modern era have competed there. The wonderful stories of Ben Hogan's triumphs and losses, Gene Sarazen's double eagle, Ken Venturi's and Charlie Coe's near-wins as amateurs, Arnold Palmer's charges, Jack Nicklaus's comeback at the age of forty-six, Seve Ballesteros's splash on 15, which cost him the victory in 1986, Bobby Jones, Byron Nelson, Sam Snead, Jimmy Demaret, Jack Burke, the losses of Greg Norman and the wins of Nick Faldo. The stories are nearly endless.

Augusta's National's uniqueness as the only permanent home for a major has contributed greatly to the rich vein of lore. The chance for new heroics happens every year. The nature of the course itself has supplied the opportunity for much of the excitement. Nowhere do you find such a blend of offensive and defensive holes. Each year, the last nine holes highlight that drama. The roller-coaster excitement of potential disaster at holes 10, 11, and 12 is punctuated by the prospect of redemption with birdies and eagles at holes 13 and 15, leaving the viewers and the golfing competitors breathless. It's very different from the other majors when making par on every hole is a challenge and a feat. At Augusta National you are avoiding train wrecks at one moment while trying to pull off a glorious shot the next.

The first time I played Augusta National, the experience was one of the few events in my life that exceeded my expectations. All the shot-making difficulties that I had envisioned were there as expected. What I wasn't prepared for was the beauty of the course. It is stunning, breathtaking, awesome. The stage is so immense and grand that you understand the great theater that happens here. There is no such thing as an ordinary round. The golf is fabulous, the environment is nearly overpowering, and the walk is constantly through history.

The course itself was about the way I had believed, except for the greens. The putting was far more difficult than I was prepared for. On the first hole I had played a nice drive and second shot just past the hole, which was cut on the middle left portion of the putting surface. Since I was above the cup, I knew it would be fast, but when my caddy informed me that I needed to play approximately twelve to fifteen feet of break to the left of the hole, I was dismayed. I could see that the putt broke to the right, but that far, no way! I was lamenting that in my first round at Augusta National I had drawn a caddy who clearly was delusional or hung over. For his benefit, I doubled my estimation of the break to about five feet to the left and tapped the putt down the slope. To my horror, I watched as the putt went absolutely sideways to the right and continued off the green and down the slope, leaving me a difficult pitch for par. Welcome to Augusta National, and apologies to my caddy. I learned quite quickly how important precision on iron shots into pin locations really is. If you are in the wrong place on the green, as my caddy said more than one time, "You're kind of dead here."

There are some holes at Augusta National where the driving area is generous, but for the most part the tee shots are demanding. In summary, I believe that anyone who is fortunate enough to play Augusta National quickly understands the reason the Masters is the favorite major and the most exciting. Everything about the course is grander and greater than you can imagine.

Jim Hardy is one of golf's most talented instructors, a frequent guest on the Golf Channel, a contributor to Golf Digest magazine, and the author of the best-selling book, The Plane Truth for Golfers.

BEN CRENSHAW AND
PLUMB-BOBBING AT AUGUSTA

John Andrisani

THE TWO-TIME MASTERS champion Ben Crenshaw is recognized for having one of the best putting strokes ever—a real necessity when playing Augusta National.

Ben Crenshaw won his first of two Masters in 1984, two years after I left England for New York City to begin working as instruction editor for *Golf Magazine*. (Crenshaw won his second Masters in 1995.)

Ben was one of the magazine's playing editors; Johnny Miller, Peter Jacobsen, Greg Norman, Seve Ballesteros, Ray Floyd, and Bobby Clampett were also among our most loyal and knowledgeable playing editors. Each year the editor, George Peper, and I would host a roundtable discussion and luncheon for this group of editors in Ponte Vedra, Florida, during the week of the Tournament Players' Championship. These get-togethers gave us an opportunity to exchange and explore ideas for articles and to enjoy listening to and telling stories.

When the subjects of golf history and putting came up, everyone turned to "Gentle Ben" Crenshaw, knowing that he was the most scholarly student of the game and a player with one of one of the best darn putting strokes ever. It was no surprise, then, when I got a chance to talk to Ben about the Augusta National golf course—during those ROUND-TABLES, at PGA Tour events, and at a restaurant in Boston during U.S. Open week, in 1988, when the venue was the Country Club in Brookline, Massachusetts—he spoke respectfully about the brilliant design of Alister MacKenzie, particularly about how this transplanted Scot collaborated with the legendary golfer Bob Jones to create a masterpiece cut out of the natural terrain, marked by the short, 155-yard 12th hole—which Ben called a "terror" and the "hardest hole in golf." Crenshaw repeated these same words when paying homage to MacKenzie, who in the fall of 2005 was inducted into golf's Hall of Fame.

As can be expected, putting played a huge role in Crenshaw's two Masters wins, for judging the speed and break in the greens is of more paramount significance at Augusta National than anywhere else. Crenshaw told me that he does not remember plumb-bobbing as often anywhere else as he did at Augusta, where the breaks in the greens are so subtle they can fool the naked eye.

Just in case you ever realize your dream of playing Augusta, or play a course with fast and sloped greens, here's how to plumb-bob Crenshaw style: Stand with your body perpendicular to the horizon and hold your putter at arm's length in front of you with only your thumb and forefinger securing the top of the grip, letting gravity ensure that the club hangs vertically. Cover the ball with the lower part of the shaft, then close your nondominant eye. If the shaft now appears also to cover the hole, the putt is straight. If the shaft appears to be to the left of the hole, the putt will break from left to right. If the shaft appears to be to the right of the hole, the putt will break from right to left.

One more tip to handling Augusta's greens and getting the ball to roll more smoothly along your intended line: like Crenshaw, swing the putter on an inside-square-inside path, just as you should your driver, not straight back and straight through, as is commonly recommended by golf instructors.

Ben Crenshaw is recognized as one of golf's avid historians, who added his name to the history books upon winning the 1984 and 1995 Masters Tournaments.

CHAPTER
18

Yes, Sir, Colonel

Brian McCallen

ONE OF THE first things I did when I landed the job as travel editor of *Golf Magazine* in October 1987 was arrange to attend the Masters the following spring. My boss, George Peper, the magazine's editor, hemmed and hawed. The only way I could attend the storied event as an accredited member of the media would be to impersonate the equipment editor, who would be leaving on Wednesday after the Par-3 Tournament preceding the main event. This was back in the days when the media credential consisted of a green metal button with a pin on the back. No heavy security, no photo identification required. I said okay. A house had been rented for the editorial team, likewise vehicles for driving to and from the club.

Like everyone who goes to Augusta National for the first time, I was struck by the scale of the place, its refinement and perfection, and the discreet peek it offered into the upper echelons of southern society. After walking the course the morning of the first round, I decided to explore the upstairs portion of the clubhouse. There, in the Champions' Locker Room, reserved for past winners of the Masters, sat the 1982 winner, Craig Stadler. He sat alone on a bench, with a newspaper resting on his crossed leg, reading it by the sunlight that streamed through the window. I wandered to the front of the building to the verandah, which nearly juts into the canopy of the great oak on the back lawn. There to my left sat Gene Sarazen, resplendent in his plus fours and two-tone spectator shoes. He was talking to Ken Venturi, who was leaning up against the rail, smoking a cigarette, and giggling. They seemed to be having a good laugh about something that happened a long time ago.

After walking around the Augusta course until three in the afternoon, taking in views of each hole and letting pictures of each register in my brain, I started searching for my fellow editors. There were none to be found in or outside the media headquarters. It turned out that the boss was an early bird who typically arrived at the crack of dawn and left after lunch. The last car had already departed for the magazine's rented house in the Augusta suburbs. I was stuck.

I wandered out into the grassy parking lot and ran into

Dick Taylor, the late golf scribe, who was a fixture in southern golf circles. I related my predicament. "Well, Brian, I'm not going in that direction, but let me introduce you to my friend the Colonel. He's right here." We walked up the center row of cars to a pearl-white Coupe de Ville convertible with the trunk open. There were ten to fifteen people standing around the spotless Cadillac. It seemed the Colonel knew everyone in the Augusta circle.

Dick introduced me to the Colonel, then told him I needed a ride home. "Have a beer, son. We'll get to that later," said the Colonel in a commanding voice. Deep in the trunk was a case of Budweiser on ice. I helped myself.

When the case ran dry, and when most of the cars in the lot were gone, the Colonel told me to hop into the car. I did as told. Our first stop was the Green Jacket, a popular restaurant and watering hole that does brisk business during Masters week. As we approached the porte cochere the Colonel jammed on the brakes. "Hey, Squire!" he yelled at the top of his lungs. Sure enough, the dapper Sarazen was slowly making his way to the entrance. He stopped and turned. The Colonel leaped out of the car without opening the door and ran to the old pro like a frantic 36-handi-capper in need of a quick swing fix. Even from sixty feet away, I could see Sarazen looking at my new friend quizzi-cally, nodding his head, smiling his wry smile, and pre-tending to remember that the Colonel was one of the first to congratulate him on his epic double eagle in 1935. The grin on the Colonel's face as he returned to the car was worth the whole trip and every bit as memorable as Sandy Lyle's fantastic fairway bunker shot on the final hole of the championship; it set up his unforgettable winning birdie putt and prompted the quiet Scot to perform a little jig on the final green.

Brian McCallen, formerly the senior travel editor at Golf Magazine, *is currently a regular contributor to* Golf Connoisseur, Travel & Leisure Golf, *and* Links. *An avid golfer, McCallen has traveled the world writing about great golf courses. His books include* Golf Resorts of the World, Top 100 Courses You Can Play, *and, most recently,* Emerging Golf Destinations. *McCallen also appears on CNN and PGA Tour radio as a golf and travel expert.*

SOUTHERN HOSPITALITY

John Andrisani

SAM SNEAD, A legendary golfer, is a three-time Masters winner whom I have had the pleasure of sitting down with on several occasions, to talk about golf. I talked to Sam once while in Helsinki, Finland, when I was a guest on a trip involving golf matches between American and Scandinavian hockey players, and "Slammin Sam" conducted a clinic at midnight when it was lights out. And I chatted with him three times in three different years during Masters week at Augusta.

One year, Snead had gotten hurt in a car accident but still showed up and was willing to sit and talk over a drink.

Since we were in the clubhouse, while outside the Masters was going on, I took the opportunity to ask him abut his wins in 1949, the year I was born, 1952, and 1954.

Snead acknowledged that he gained the greatest satisfaction from winning in 1954, when he beat the previous year's winner, Ben Hogan, in an eighteen-hole playoff. I expected Snead to say that, knowing that the two were rivals; Snead, the natural swinger, vs. Hogan, the mechanical golfer. What I did not expect was the answer he gave me when I asked him point-blank: "What makes Augusta such a revered domain among professional golfers, even the most critical ones such as you?"

Snead's answer: "More than the greatness of the course, it's the greatness of the Augusta members, which at all times do what they once did or still do in the real world: think intelligently, plan ahead, delegate, firmly demand perfection, and work hard to be the best at what they do. The result is the Masters, a tournament that runs like a Rolls Royce engine, as smooth and effective as my swing."

Snead went on to tell me that although winning the Masters was always his priority, he never lost sleep over losing. The gallery and the press were kept under such control that all he had to do was concentrate on playing golf. Besides, he felt at home at Augusta National, and had fun enjoying the challenge of testing his skills against the course, as well as drinking, eating, and joking around with the gallery and his fellow pros and members.

Sam Snead is regarded by most golf experts, including Tiger Woods's former coach John Anselmo, as the all-time greatest swinger of a club.

Knock-Knock

Peter Peck

CERTAIN SITUATIONS IN life in which one finds oneself can bring back a memory, a feeling, or sensation one has previously experienced. Such was the case when I first played Augusta National.

Immediately after I walked through the doors of the clubhouse, which open to the vista of the course, I was awed. I had the exact same feeling, I thought, when as a child I went to Yankee Stadium for the first time. The same sense of deepness of colors, the almost surreal vista that unfolded before me, made me feel as if I were in a museum surrounded by paintings by masters. The feeling was virtually too perfect to be real, and the aura of Augusta was so much stronger when I was standing on the course than when, as a young boy, I watched players competing on it on television. Just as when watching ballplayers whom I worshipped at Yankee Stadium, when watching the game's best golfers at Augusta I was so electrified that it I felt as if I were floating on a cloud.

What came as another surprise was that—more than the greatness of the course, its history, and the wonderful surroundings—it was the staff that runs Augusta National that left an indelible mark on my brain.

The first year I attended the Masters I stayed in one of the club's handsome cabins. When I felt like having a cup of coffee, lunch, an afternoon cocktail—and I am not lying when I say this—the second I had such a yearning, there was a knock at the door. When I opened it, a staff member appeared, as if popping from a genie's lamp, and asked me if I would like what I desired. This should give you a hint of how well trained and instinctually knowledgeable the Augusta staff is about human nature and timing; they read the wishes of members and guests as expertly as the caddies read the greens.

I first visited Augusta at a time when the pros competing in the championship used the "house caddies," not their own, and Freddie Bennett was designated the "Caddy Master." Freddie and all the caddies had a strong bond to the club, namely because they worked for the members and truly knew the layout of the course like the backs of their hands. Moreover, they were up on the history of Augusta and loved sharing it with first-timers like me.

Freddie in particular was there to treat guests with

kindness and efficiency. He filled in the canvas of Augusta with a fine brush, leaving out nothing important, but keeping some things to himself, most notably the story of the morning when he found Clifford Roberts dead on the golf course. Apparently, Roberts, having found out that there was nothing more his doctor could do for him, put a gun to his head in a place he called home. (I was told more details about Roberts by Freddie, such as where he is buried, but as a gesture of respect to the club, I asked John Andrisani to please leave these out, and he agreed that it was the right thing to do.)

Few of our American golf clubs can boast a history such as Augusta National's, and it was best told by the caddies— especially by good old Freddie, who is now retired. However, on my first visit, he took me around the course one afternoon to all the places where great shots had been hit by professionals competing in the Masters. Freddie had a knack for giving you the flavor, not just the facts. For that matter, all of the caddies did a pretty good job of that; making you feel like a member for the day. And, trust me, there is no place better to be a member than Augusta National Golf Club. I know that, having just gotten a taste of the golf course, the food, the wine, the history, and most of all the stories told to me by the caddies. The humanity of this American institution has no equal in the world of golf.

Peter Peck, senior vice president of UBS Financial Services, Inc., in New York City, is a member of the Meadowbrook Golf Club in Long Island, New York, and an extremely passionate golfer who has played many of the world's top-ranked courses.

CHAPTER
21

A Good Laugh

Don Trahan

ALTHOUGH I HAD been fortunate enough to attend the Masters Tournament several times before 2001, in that year I came to see everything from an entirely different perspective. In 2001, my son, D.J. Trahan (now a PGA Tour player), whom I had taught how to play golf, received an invitation to play in the Masters—the tournament of tournaments, as I call it—by virtue of winning the 2000 U.S. Amateur Public Links championship.

D.J.'s formal invitation included unlimited playing-time rights. In short, he sort of became an Augusta member, with his privileges extending right up until the time of the event, April 2001. All D.J. had to do during this stretch of time was call up the pro shop at Augusta let a staff member know when he planned to visit. He could have played every day and all day long. Furthermore, D.J.'s privileges at Augusta National allowed him to invite one guest each visit, who could not play but was allowed to go everywhere on the premises with him. This included the dining room, where I fell in love with the house soup—a kind of clam bisque is the way I remember it, but very special indeed, and that's coming from the mouth of a seafood-loving Massachusetts native. So special is that bisque, in fact, that I'm still trying to pull some strings to get the recipe.

During his "membership" time, D.J. simply charged everything to an account and I received statements from the club that I made sure to pay promptly. Boy, did he take advantage of this opportunity, playing a lot of golf and inviting a number of guests. He invited me, my brother, friends from his high school, and the coaches from Clemson, the college he attended. Thanks to D.J., we all got a true insider's look into the Augusta National Golf Club.

What impressed me most was how when D.J. went round the course, the members stepped aside and took the time to welcome him to Augusta.

I was excited when Dave Spencer, the head professional of Augusta National at the time, complimented me on how good a job I had done in helping D.J. to construct a powerfully controlled three-quarter swing action. I laughed, telling Spencer that D.J. was so afraid of digging turf out of the perfectly manicured silky green fairways that he actually bladed a few shots. D.J. soon made up for that, though, by going to the driving range and blasting several balls over the net at the back of the range.

The week after the tournament, the April 16, 2001, issue of *Sports Illustrated* ran an article in the publication's "Notebook" department entitled "Screen Monster," written by Jamie Diaz, which told how the net was raised during Masters week. That happened because after witnessing D.J.'s feat prior to the tournament, Masters officials feared bombers such as D.J. and Tiger Woods would knock balls into the windshields of cars driving on Washington Road, which runs behind the range.

I found the whole story of D.J.'s power-hitting extremely amusing, yet the most ironic anecdote involves what I observed in the men's room of the locker room. Instead of seeing on the walls magnificent photographs, watercolors, and oil paintings of Augusta's great golf holes, in front of my eyes were caricature pictures of canines, including one showing dogs standing in line to pee on a fire hydrant. So, those of you who perceive Augusta's members as stuck up, stuffy, rich old men owe them an apology. Like the rest of us, they obviously have a good sense of humor. You'd need one, too, if you had to play as tough a course as Augusta on a regular basis.

Don Trahan is one of the best golf instructors in America and is the father of the PGA Tour player D.J. Trahan.

CHAPTER
22

Sandy Lyle's Memorable Moments with Jack Nicklaus

John Andrisani

SANDY LYLE, WHOM I have had the pleasure of inter-viewing and playing golf with, won the 1988 Masters by scoring birdie on the seventy-second hole, after hitting a miraculous fairway bunker shot and holing a pressure putt.

My relationship with Sandy Lyle goes back a long time, and it's important to share our history together to appre-ciate more fully his love of Augusta National Golf Club, and the reason he won a green jacket.

In America, during the 1977 Walker Cup Matches, a biennial contest between an amateur team from the United States and an amateur squad from Great Britain and Ireland,

Sandy Lyle, a youngster from Shrewsbury, England, with an impressive swing and an equally creditable demeanor, caught my eye. He was just nineteen, however, so I dismissed from my mind any thoughts of putting an asterisk alongside his name, for things could transpire down the road, and had done before to other promising players. Besides, surely his fearless swing was simply a symptom of a youthful lack of inhibition; his excellent temperament, the sign of a shy teenager.

What would become of this young man once he turned professional and fell victim to the pressure of Tour golf? What would happen to his free-flowing rhythm once a teacher started dissecting his swing? Would his adherence to sound fundamentals come unstuck once he was tempted with trendy swing theories? I pondered these thoughts upon leaving the venue for the competition, which that year was Shinnecock Hills Golf Club in Southampton, on Long Island.

Not long after the Walker Cup Matches, I departed the United States for England, and settled into a job as assistant editor at *Golf Illustrated*. Eventually, in August 1979, I caught up with Sandy Lyle at Hawkstone Park, his home club in Shropshire, England.

Sandy had already won on the professional circuit. His swing still ran as efficiently as a Bentley and still looked effortless. The only difference I could see in Sandy's game was that he had put numerous new shots into his repertoire and had an even keener understanding of what makes a first-class technique tick. It was obvious to me that Sandy's own imaginative powers, plus the swing secrets passed on to him by his father, Alex Lyle, had helped him mature as a golfer.

During my stay at *Golf Illustrated*, Sandy and I had the opportunity to play golf together and talk technique for hours at a time.

In late 1982 I moved to New York to work as senior editor of instruction at *Golf Magazine*.

In 1984, Sandy and I connected again. Through his agent, Mark McCormack, he arranged for us to meet at Bay Hill Golf Club in Orlando, Florida, where we embarked on a project together: a golf-instruction book. Two years later, in 1986, after many heavy discussions and lengthy taping sessions with Sandy, *Learning Golf: The Lyle Way* was published.

While Sandy and I collaborated on this book, the subject of major championships came up. One of his dreams, he told me, was to win the Masters Tournament; moreover, he believed that this dream would come true because the look of Augusta National, with its hills and beautiful tree-lined fairways, reminded him of Hawkstone Park. I believed anything was possible, considering Sandy had already won the 1985 British Open Championship.

Well, in 1988, Sandy's dream of winning the Masters came true, following a miraculous shot from a fairway bunker and a perfect birdie putt on the final hole.

I was joyous about Sandy's victory, but it wasn't until touching base with Sandy at different PGA Tour venues around America and conversing with him about Augusta National that I learned the main reason behind his spectacular win. Here is the explanation Sandy gave me, which, I admit, I never expected: "Playing in the final round of the 1986 Masters with Jack Nicklaus, and listening to the roars of the gallery and living through the tension and excitement as Nicklaus hit great shot after great shot en route to winning his sixth Masters, readied me to win.

"That experience allowed me to get a sense of what it takes to deal with the highly intense down-the-stretch pressure you feel on day four of the Masters and how to handle it."

Sandy Lyle has two major championship victories to his credit—the 1985 British Open and the 1988 Masters.

CHAPTER
23

TRUE PERFECTION

Joseph A. DeLuca

GROWING UP IN Wilmington, Delaware and being introduced to the game of golf, I was aware of the Masters and,
of course, of the very special place where it is held, Augusta
National, the venue for my favorite major championship.

Terl Johnson, my home professional at the Dupont
Country Club was a contestant in the Masters one year,
having gone to the quarter finals in the PGA Championship, then a match-play event. So I was invited to watch
him compete and have the opportunity to engross myself in
the Augusta experience.

I knew Augusta National Golf Club was a special place,
but being there exceeded my expectations, as there truly is

nothing like it that I know of in the world of golf. Hats off to the creators, Bobby Jones and Alister MacKenzie.

Once walking the course, the colors of the flowers, trees, water, fairways, and greens—yellow, pearl white, bright green, pink—made me feel as if I were looking at an Impressionist painting by Claude Monet.

In continuing my observations, I could see that the participants were in awe of the place, just as I was. The grand clubhouse, the quaint guest cottages, the cute par-3 course, the sounds of water running through the meandering Rae's Creek—everything made me feel as if I were in a dreamland. The more time I spent scrutinizing every nook and cranny at Augusta, the more it seemed that only one word could do justice to it: *perfection*. I told this to the past president of the Professional Golfers Association of America, Leo Fraser, who told me that even the soap, toilet paper, and towels in the locker room are of the highest quality, and there is an attendant available to cater to everyone's needs.

The bottom line: Augusta National is golf's showplace and a testimony to the greatness of the game. My advice: Somehow, someway, find a way to get there one day, since you will remember the experience for the rest of your life. Honestly, not a day goes by that I don't think back and realize how lucky I was to walk around a course where golf's greatest players have made their mark on history.

Joseph A. DeLuca, a longtime golf teacher, is president of the Golf Instruction Club Network, designed to help member-players improve on a steady basis at clubs across America. He is also the innovator of the best-selling DVD The Great Golf Hoax Exposed.

CHAPTER
24

The Importance of Being a Good Chipper at Augusta

John Andrisani

During my sixteen-year stint as instruction editor for *Golf Magazine*, from 1982 to 1998, I worked with many top professionals on articles designed to help our readers play better golf. I consider myself one of the luckiest men alive to be able to write about a sport I love and learn from the pros and pass on their teachings to other golfers. Each and every pro had something new and fresh to say. And when it came to discussions on short-game technique, namely chipping, no pro golfer had more interesting things to say than Ray Floyd. Throughout his PGA Tour career, during which he won three major championships—the

1969 PGA, the 1976 Masters, and the 1986 U.S. Open—Floyd proved himself to be one of the game's best shot makers whose art for getting the ball up and in (or holing out) from around the greens was no less than phenomenal.

In the mid-1980s, I was working on a article about chipping with Ray. Ray is a player who essentially chips like he putts, using his arms to control the movement of the club, yet he does depend on a slight hinging of the wrists to promote feel. I asked him how important a role the chip shot played in his Masters win.

"John, if a player doesn't chip the ball well at Augusta, he cannot win," said Floyd. "The reason is that the greens are fast running, sloped, and angular in shape, so you are bound to miss a few on your approach shots. Therefore, if you do not have the ability to use your imagination to 'see' the right type of chip shot play out in your mind's eye, choose the correct club to hit the shot, employ the right technique, and swing the club at the right speed, gently or more briskly, you will leave yourself a long par putt or another chip!"

Whether you ever play Augusta or not, Floyd's words should tell you how vitally important it is to practice chipping with a variety of clubs, with the goal of lofting the ball over the fringe and getting it to roll like a putt as soon as possible after landing. If you follow Ray's example, you will be prepared for any course situation—hopefully, some of them at Augusta National during your dream round.

Raymond Floyd, a Champions Tour player and former PGA Tour superstar, is a short-game ace who has won golf tournaments all over the world, including the 1976 Masters.

CHAPTER
25

THE WRONG APPROACH

Mike Dunaway

MY EXPERIENCE PLAYING Augusta National came at the invitation of an Augusta member; a famous gentleman whose name I'd rather keep private. Needless to say, it was a special trip. The best way to truly appreciate the wonder of Augusta is to visit it, and I hope you do. Let me share with you some highlights of my own special Augusta experience, which I hope will give you a sense of being there.

My first thoughts as I turned down Magnolia Lane and then a short time after observed the practice range, was whether or not I could knock the ball over its high net, which is nearly three hundred yards away. Later, I teed up a dozen balls and knocked all but one over the fence.

I played fifty-four holes over two days, my goal being to find one weed and bring it home. The reason I say that is because I had heard how impeccably manicured Augusta was, but knew that there had to be at least one weed growing on the course, which formerly had been a nursery. What happened? I found not one foreign blade of grass on the entire Augusta property.

Being a long driver, I couldn't wait to hit some solid tee shots on the course and compare them to those hit by Tour players. Well, I did hit many drives over three hundred yards, which delighted me. However, the funniest moment came on the par-5 8th hole. After reaching my drive I asked my caddy, who had carried the bags of top Tour players, what club to hit for my second shot. His answer: "After seeing how far you hit the ball, I have no idea, man."

As easy as I found the driving, owing largely to hitting to fairways that were surprisingly wide compared to many other championship courses, I found the approach shots to elevated undulated greens extremely difficult. For example, on the second day, when playing the 3rd hole, a short par-4, I only had thirty yards left to the green. However, because I was indecisive about what club to hit, a sand wedge or lob wedge, and failed to commit to a specific type of shot, I hit the ball over the green and ended up scoring six on the hole. I also lost confidence in my wedge game. At that point, I understood why Augusta is such a painfully difficult course to score on.

The chief reason approach shots are so difficult is that the fairways are very tight, so you have to be careful not to skull the ball (hit it with the leading edge of the club instead of the sweet spot of the club face). I did that on hole number three, since I was used to hitting the ball off the lush fairways at my home club, Pinnacle Country Club in Rogers, Arkansas.

My advice to those of you who are lucky enough to play Augusta: on short iron shots, think hard about club selection, visualize the shot you want to play, commit to that shot, and hit down on the ball with a sharp descending blow.

Regardless of the state of the course, now more difficult owing to added length and deeper rough bordering the fairways, you will have fun playing Augusta National, a strategic course that rewards good shots and punishes you severely for gambling and failing to hit the shot you planned to hit.

Mike Dunaway is former winner of the World Super Long Drive Contest. He employs what Ken Venturi, a two-time runner-up in the Masters Tournament, once called "the most powerfully accurate swing in golf."

CHAPTER
26

Beauty and the Beast

John Andrisani

GARY PLAYER, WHOM I've had the pleasure of interviewing on several occasions, won the Masters Tournament in 1961, 1974, and 1978.

I've been traveling the world interviewing Tour professionals and writing about golf for nearly thirty years (all of my previous books have been instructional in nature). While working for *Golf Magazine*, from 1982 to 1998, I sometimes was asked to fly off to a destination to review a new course (in fact, today, I still review courses for *Sarasota* magazine in Sarasota, Florida). Moreover, having played the game for forty-nine years, I've teed up the ball on all types of courses and talked to top course architects about their work. Therefore, I have a good idea of the criteria required for calling a course a great course. Obviously, though, my expertise doesn't go deep enough to be comparable with that of the legendary golfer and course designer Gary Player. I've had the opportunity to work with Player on a number of instructional articles and to talk to him about great golf courses around the world.

Probably the most profound statement made by Player about golf was a quip he made some thirty years ago, which is now part of golf lore and goes something like this: "If there is a golf course in Heaven, it must be another Augusta National."

When I spoke to Gary, what must be nearly twenty years ago, in the clubhouse of Alaqua Golf Club in central Florida, he reiterated this assessment. I took the opportunity to ask him why the Augusta National course is so special.

He responded, "Augusta is ingeniously laid out so that it looks easy, but it's a wolf in sheep's clothing.

"Holes six, twelve and sixteen, all par-threes, are quite short, yet hazards that border the tricky greens make scoring difficult.

"The par-four holes feature greens that lend themselves to placing the flagsticks in very testing positions. Therefore, if you land the ball well above the hole, you will face a treacherous downhill putt that forces you to play defensively to try and save par.

"The par fives are short enough to reach in two. The tendency is to gamble and go for the green rather than lay up. This type of strategic choice, particularly on holes thirteen and fifteen, can cause you to land in Rae's Creek and shoot such a high score that you are behind the eight ball.

"What I'm saying is every hole at Augusta is a great hole, because you must think, think, think and never doubt your choice of club or shot. Consequently, mental stamina is a must for success at August National."

Gary Player is one of only six players to win all four major championships, as well as a world-renowned course architect and ambassador for the game of golf.

CHAPTER
27

FLYING HIGH

John Andrisani

SOME OF THE most memorable moments of my golf
writing career involved working with PGA tour player Fred
Couples first on articles for *Golf Magazine*, then later on
the book *Total Shotmaking: The Golfer's Guide to Low
Scoring*, which we collaborated on in 1994.

During our time together, as we discussed the content of
the book and the game of golf in general and as I watched him
play and practice, I soon learned that Fred is a super-talented
tee-to-green shot-maker who possesses an inner competitive
fire that he successfully hides from the public, although his
fellow pro golfers are fully aware of his killer instinct.

When the subject of Fred's 1992 Masters victory came up, his eyes lit up because he took pride in knowing that since that monumental win he no longer was being called "the best player never to win a major."

Because Fred is not an egotist, he shared credit for his win with others, not only the golf instructor Paul Marchand, but also the late golf teacher Dick Harmon. Dick was the man who passed on to Fred shot-making secrets that he had learned from his father, Claude Harmon, Sr., the winner of the 1948 Masters.

En route to his eventual victory in Augusta, Fred played well over seventy-two holes of competition, and he needed to play all kinds of shots. But, according to him, other than the chip he played on hole number twelve in the final round, the type of shot that played the single biggest role in his shooting the winning score of 275 was the lofted-iron approach shot. This shot is particularly advantageous when an approach requires a long or medium iron into the green. In contrast, a shot hit low will hit the green and "chase" into trouble, namely a bunker.

Dick Harmon knew how to play this shot, having learned it from his dad, and he simply passed on swing tips to Fred.

If you're lucky enough to play golf at Augusta National, you'll also need to hit this shot, so let me teach you the secrets to success that I learned from Fred:

In setting up, play the ball high up off your left instep, grip the club lightly, put slightly more weight on your right foot, and keep your head well behind the ball.

Start the club back from the ball very slowly, concentrating on making a full shoulder turn and setting the club softly at the top.

Strive for a slow, smooth transition into the downswing, turning the hips fully through the impact zone. Release the club freely through the ball rather than hitting at it. The goal is to hit the ball on the upswing so that a little loft is added to the club face. Focus on the loose re-cocking of the club-head, up and to the left. Continue on into a full, balanced follow-through.

Tailoring the tip: According to Fred, when hitting to a very small target, namely, a limited flat area of grass on a very undulating green (as occurs often at Augusta National), add even a little more stopping power by adjusting your stance to just a touch open, to put a trace of fade-spin on the ball.

In late December 2005, Fred, then forty-nine, appeared on the Golf Channel to tell golfers about the new added-length changes to the Augusta National course and the clubs he had to use to hit into them. He told viewers that he felt he could conceivably win another Masters, giving as his reason the fact that he has the length to handle the newly lengthened course. "I'm hitting the ball longer than ever," said Fred.

When I heard him say that he hit a two-iron to the par-3 fourth hole and a three-wood for his second shot at hole 11, I realized that the course as newly tuned is now going to play into the hands of boomers like Freddie. Many golf professionals just will not have a chance to win. And don't even think about blaming Augusta. The membership really had little choice but to lengthen the course, considering that today's new drivers allow golfers to hit the ball longer than ever. Personally, I'd like to see the courses—particularly one that embodies as much history and tradition as Augusta—stay the same.

The veteran PGA Tour player Fred Couples is nicknamed Boom Boom because he hits high, powerful shots from the tee and off fairways onto greens. He is best known for his win at the 1992 Masters.

CHAPTER
28

SOMETIMES THE CAMERA DOES LIE

Nick Mastroni

PERHAPS I AM dating myself rather unflatteringly by recalling that my first visit to Augusta National was some twenty-four years ago, in April 1982. That year I cashed in one of my perks as a member of the *Golf Magazine* editorial staff—attending the Masters.

Seeing Augusta in the flesh was something I had craved for many years. I had watched the Masters Tournament on television every April, religiously, for as long as I could recall—at least back to 1961. That year, I remember the cameras jumping back and forth between Arnold Palmer playing the final hole, and Gary Player anxiously watching him on the screen from inside the clubhouse. Player had just finished shooting 74 and had given up the lead to Palmer. But Palmer scored double bogey at the last (after a perfect drive), and so handed the title back to the South African, who aside from playing a heck of a game of golf was known for often dressing in black.

It took a couple of more decades, but at last I could see for myself the competitive venue which had been the backdrop for so much high golfing drama. I was not at all disappointed, and I learned that the television cameras could not begin to tell the whole story of Augusta National. I will admit, however, that I was a little taken aback that first morning when I and my companions drove to the club. Washington Road, the main east–west thoroughfare through the city of Augusta, was crowded with commercial hodgepodge, belying its status as an approach to a property as lordly as Augusta National. In fact, I recall being surprised when we actually just made the turn into Magnolia Lane. I guess I had expected an out-of-the-ordinary transition from such everyday surrounding and dealings to such an extraordinary place.

Once inside, you find Augusta National to be fabulous, no matter whether you are critiquing it as a golf club or an architectural exemplar or for its history, the unsurpassed beauty of the course and the surrounding flora, its immaculate conditioning, the meticulous manner in which its administration conducts the championship, or the challenges and difficulties of the fabled course. As for me, I'm a meat-and-potatoes golf course guy. Others are certainly far more familiar with and interested in recalling the clubhouse, the locker rooms, the food, the social elements, and so forth. I just remember the awe I felt as I traipsed along while trying to drink in the nuances of each of the eighteen holes.

The first thing that struck me upon seeing Augusta is just how hilly the course is. Despite the steadily advancing sophistication of video technology, a television screen simply cannot do justice to Augusta National's swooping terrain. From the high ground in front of the clubhouse, you can see clearly how steeply uphill the approach shot to the 18th green is. No wonder the trek up the ultimate fairway used to be known as Heartbreak Hill. You can also see how sharply the 10th hole dives downhill from the tee and bends dramatically left toward the green.

As I took in the entire course it became apparent that just about every hole presents the problem of a shot that must be struck from a significantly uphill, downhill, or side-hill lie. If the shot is from a level fairway lie (or from the tee), it still needs to go up a steep hill to the green, as at the par-4 7th, or downhill, as at the par-3 6th, or when you are going for the green in two shots at the par-5 15.

Of course, I was aware from listening to others who'd been to Augusta that a key to winning or even being in the running in the Masters was the player's ability to place the approach shots in precise spots just below the many fiendish pin placements, in order to give birdie putts even a reasonable chance. When I coupled the need for such a fine degree of precision on approach shots with the fact the most of these approaches were played from some type of substantially slanted lie and stance—well, I guess you could say that the light bulb went on. Everyone knows how slick and treacherous Augusta National's greens are, but I think this additional shot-making wrinkle is one of the hidden reasons why Augusta National has been so resistant to really low scoring. There is little I can add to what has been said by others of situations where these perplexing approach shots must carry the water that jealously guards the greens, as at holes 11, 12, 13, 15, and 16. However, I feel compelled to contribute a further observation: You probably have heard of how golf-course architects often try to design holes for the members that will "look hard and play easy." I think the holes Alister MacKenzie and Bobby Jones created at Augusta National were designed to look easy and play hard. The course just looks so inviting, until you have to actually hit the shots to overcome its baffling nuances.

A word is in order about how much Augusta National has been changed over the years in order to keep up with the massive advances in playing equipment and, yes, players' increasing athleticism as well. Those who have become golf fans fairly recently might be led to believe that Augusta National of 1982, which played at about 6,900 yards, must have been an overhyped cakewalk. After all, some of today's PGA Tour courses stretch to over 7,500 yards, and indeed, Augusta National's most recent refinements have it now measuring 7,445 yards. But things were really quite different back then. Those newfangled "metal woods" were only gaining the public's attention in the early eighties. In 1982, I would guess that although some Tour players had switched over to metal, they were still a minority. And keep in mind that because those early metal-wood designs were made of steel rather than today's lightweight titanium, the club heads were still roughly similar in size to the old "wood" woods—that is, well under half the size of the ultralight, 400 cc–plus warheads that Tiger Woods, Phil Mickelson, and Vijay Singh use to launch their 340-yard blasts. In the same vein, I would guess that most Tour players of that era were still hitting the traditional muscle-back-blade-style irons as compared to the more forgiving cavity-backs. And most would concur that today's golf ball alone is worth ten to twenty yards more off the tee (and nearly as much off the irons) than the top models of a quarter century ago. Which is all to say that the Augusta National I experienced in 1982 could very well have been more daunting to players than the current course— Augusta's 500-plus yards of new length and the addition of its "second cut" (which would be referred to as "light rough") notwithstanding.

In the practice rounds before that 1982 Masters, I recall that the course was playing hard and fast. Back then some of the players howled that no one would even match par unless some rain came through to soften the course. Well, the players got their wish, along with a very different set of problems during Thursday's opening round. It poured miserably all day and there was a chill in the air to boot. Suddenly, the course went from playing race-track fast to playing very, very long. I remember standing at the 9th green while Tom Kite and Jerry Pate approached their tee shots below. On this sweeping dogleg-left, the slope of the fairway falls to the right, meaning that the tee shot must be drawn or the ball will wander away. Pate's ball had ended up well to the right, and even though at the time there was no rough, I estimated that he was left with a shot of 200 yards from a downhill, side-hill lie, steeply back uphill to the green. I thought Pate would have to hit a fairway wood, but he went with an iron, I would guess perhaps a number three-iron, and drilled it onto the front edge of the green. A television viewer could never fully grasp how difficult a shot that was.

A score of 75 that day was certainly not cause for cutting one's throat. As a matter of fact, that's what Craig Stadler shot. Then the front passed through and the weather turned glorious for the remaining three days of the championship. Naturally, the scores improved too, with the course playing fairly soft in rounds 2 through 4. So soft, in fact, that Stadler, who ultimately won, managed to come back from that opening 75 to finish with a three-under-par 284 total. (Dan Pohl tied Stadler after seventy-two holes, but Stadler won in a playoff.)

So, granted, the Augusta National golf course is now much longer than in days gone by. But everything is relative. In my mind, Augusta was and always will be the greatest challenge and the ultimate major championship venue.

Nick Mastroni is an editorial icon in the world of golf publishing and a low-handicap golfer. His magazine credits include associate editor, Golf Magazine; *equipment editor,* Golf Illustrated; *editor,* Golf Tips; *and senior editor (instruction),* Senior Golfer. *Mastroni, a true golf aficionado, based in Georgia, collaborated with short-game guru Dave Pelz on the golf best-seller* Putt Like the Pros.